Sir Garfield Sobers was born  the West Indies between 1965 Queen in 1975. He now lives the Barbados Tourist Board.

Brian Scovell works for the *Daily Mail*. He has known Garry Sobers since 1963, and used to 'ghost' his column worldwide.

Sir Garfield Sobers
with Brian Scovell

SOBERS
Twenty Years at the Top

Foreword by Sir Donald Bradman

PAN BOOKS
in association with
MACMILLAN

First published 1988 by Macmillan London Ltd
This edition published 1989 by Pan Books Ltd,
Cavaye Place, London SW10 9PG
in association with Macmillan
9 8 7 6 5 4 3 2 1
ISBN 0 330 30868 8

Printed and bound in Great Britain by
Richard Clay Ltd, Bungay, Suffolk

Contents

List of Illustrations

Foreword

Back in 1930/31 I played against the first West Indian cricket team to tour Australia. Included among the visitors was Learie Constantine, one of the most dynamic players of cricket history.

When his playing days were over Learie became renowned in the world of politics and on his death had become Lord Constantine, MBE.

He and I developed a close personal friendship and when he made a political trip to Australia as a member of a parliamentary delegation we exchanged at some length our respective views on matters in the cricket world.

I remember quite vividly his reference to a young West Indian named Garry Sobers who had just started to blossom in his home country.

'Don't miss this boy,' said Learie, 'he is marvellous and the hardest hitter of a ball I have ever seen.'

As Constantine himself was a ferocious hitter and not given to exaggerated statements I followed his advice and watched out for the advent of Sobers on Australian soil.

I was not disappointed. It was obvious at once that here was a boy with exceptional talent.

In my recent public appraisal of all-round cricketers I unhesitatingly rated Garry Sobers as the greatest all-rounder I ever saw.

The competition for such an accolade was awesome. There were many contenders for the title, men like Hammond, Botham, Miller, Benaud and Davidson.

I did not consider Grace, Rhodes, Woolley and others of their period simply because I did not have the chance to evaluate their skills.

Obviously they were magnificent but in every sport where there is a meaningful yardstick for comparison, the modern athlete is way ahead of the champion of yesteryear. So I feel on safe ground in broadly thinking the same has happened in cricket.

I am not going to rely on figures (impressive though they are) to support my case but am backing my judgement through visual observation.

The first thing about Sobers was his beautiful athletic build. Around six feet tall he possessed a trim, lithe body and moved with a deceptive feline grace which is so often characteristic of West Indians. Circumstances usually dictated that he should field close to the wicket but he was superb in any position.

As a bowler he handled the new ball with excellent control of swing and later in a match could bowl orthodox first-finger spin, or googlies off the third finger. This versatility made him a captain's dream even though I think it was the main reason why his total career wickets were a little more costly than those of some of his contemporaries. It is extraordinarily difficult to bowl every variety with pinpoint accuracy.

But it was in batting that his genius shone the brightest.

I shared Constantine's view of his power and nothing will ever erase from my memory two shots I saw him play.

One was on the Adelaide Oval. The bowler was Alan Davidson, a left hander of not inconsiderable pace. Alan bowled a bumper at Sobers. The ball rose roughly shoulder high and, off his back foot, with a horizontal blade, Sobers hit him over mid-on for 6, the ball landing halfway up the hill just under the scoreboard. It was simply unbelievable power.

The second was on the Melbourne Cricket Ground.

The proposed 1971–2 tour of Australia by South Africa had been cancelled and was replaced by a World XI of which Sobers was made captain.

In the third of the internationals Australia versus a World XI after the latter was already one down in the series and 101 behind on their first innings, Sobers, after having made a duck in his first innings, strode to the wicket to confront Lillee and his supports, facing apparent defeat.

From the first ball Sobers commenced an unrelenting attack on the bowling. I was sitting almost directly behind Lillee as he delivered one of his thunderbolts but Sobers unleashed the most wonderful straight drive which hit the sight-screen almost before the bowler's forward momentum had finished.

I rose from my chair to join in the spontaneous applause.

Garry finished with 254, an innings so marvellous that it was later to be the subject of a special film for which I was proud to do the commentary. It was certainly the best innings I have ever seen on Australian soil and I believe the best ever played in this country.

Without any doubt Sobers played fast bowling better than any batsman from any country. Whether it was in defence, attack or evasion, his positioning was always perfect and quite relaxed, a tribute to eyesight, co-ordination and judgement.

As an overseas player Garry was brought to Adelaide to play Sheffield Shield cricket for South Australia and in that regard I had much to do with him both as a player and an individual. He was always charming, approachable and modest and it is my pleasure to pay a tribute to a man who, as the greatest all rounder ever, gave me so much enjoyment.

It was fitting that Her Majesty the Queen should confer a knighthood on this sporting genius.

The story of his life and his rise from humble beginnings to world status is both fascinating and inspirational to cricket lovers everywhere.

Sir Donald Bradman
Adelaide
January 1988

Acknowledgements

I would like to thank Adam Sisman of Macmillan for enabling me to write about my years in cricket, Tony Cozier for helping the project at the start and providing the background and statistics, and Brian Scovell for writing the words.

I would also like to thank Tony, and also Willie Alleyne and Alrick Gaskin in Barbados, for their help in assembling the pictures.

1 | It's Still the Same Game

I would love to be still playing competitive cricket. I envy those who are currently representing the West Indies. It is said that the game has changed since I retired from Test cricket in 1974, that it is a harder game to play.

They say there are more fast bowlers bowling more short-pitched deliveries, making it difficult for batsmen to play their shots, and that the players are fitter and take more catches. They say there is more pressure because of the extra financial rewards.

The game has changed in some ways, I will concede that. There are bigger incentives for the players, more travelling and more matches to play. It is true that the players train harder than in my day. The more time you spend at catching practice, the more catches you will take. We didn't chase round the boundary and dive to stop fours as some fielders do now.

But I do not accept that it is any harder now for batsmen than it was when I was playing. In the past decade there have been more fast bowlers of quality, but most of them have retired or are nearing the end of their career. The West Indian dominance in fast bowling seems to be on the wane, temporarily at least.

Malcolm Marshall survives, the fastest and straightest of them, but Michael Holding, Joel Garner, Colin Croft and Andy Roberts have all left Test cricket. It was shown in the Reliance World Cup in India and Pakistan that their successors, Courtney Walsh, Patrick Patterson and Winston Benjamin, are still learning their craft.

Except for Patterson, who is genuinely quick, I do not think any of the new generation is as fast as the players who have departed. Surrey's Tony Gray has potential because he is the same size as Joel

Garner, whose main threat lay in the way he steepled the ball up at the batsman off a length. I think any great batsman of the past would have been troubled by 'Bird'.

Marshall, now nearing the veteran stage, may have three or four years left. For a small man he gets tremendous pace by running in fast and not hesitating as he comes to the crease. I once played for my Barbados club side, Police, against him and found him a little presumptuous. I believe he still is. I was forty at the time, and the locals were saying he was waiting for me. I enjoyed playing against him.

There is no one to take the place of Holding, who became a great bowler after taking some time to establish himself. Perhaps one of the new crop will follow his example – Walsh, perhaps, who has had a sound apprenticeship with Gloucestershire.

The lesson of the 1987 World Cup is that the pendulum is swinging back towards spin bowlers. The most successful bowlers were the spinners like Maninder Singh and John Emburey. I believe that is a good thing. Spin bowling always has been an integral part of the game. It is coming back because a generation of batsmen is emerging that has little experience of playing it. Good spin bowlers are taking wickets again.

When I was playing the Indians had four spin bowlers of world class: Bedi, Venkataraghavan, Prasanna and Chandrasekhar. For a time India was one of the most respected cricketing nations in the world, twice winning series against the West Indies.

The emergence of the West Indies as the world's best team began in Australia in 1960–1 under the late Sir Frank Worrell, the greatest captain I played under in my twenty-year career as a Test player. I was honoured to succeed him and continue his work of uniting the players from different regions of the Caribbean.

By 1963 we had the outstanding pair of fast bowlers in world cricket: Wes Hall, fast, tireless and full of the joy of bowling, and Charlie Griffith, frighteningly hostile at times and crucified by those who claimed his action was sometimes outside the laws. In 1964–5 it was said that the Australians spent hours looking at film of

Charlie's action. If they thought he threw the occasional delivery, why take hours? It should have been noticeable in a split second.

There has been no more effective West Indian fast bowler than Charlie Griffith. I would much sooner face the fast-bowling battery of Clive Lloyd's team than Charlie and Wes in their prime. Charlie's opponents queried his action because his left leg didn't land where it should have landed and he was open-chested. He didn't have a textbook action so he must have thrown, they claimed, especially when he bowled his bouncer or his deadliest ball of all, his yorker.

Well, my interpretation of a fair delivery is the one written in the laws of the game: that in the delivery the arm doesn't straighten immediately prior to the ball leaving the bowler's hand. Charlie's arm didn't straighten.

No team had as many as four fast bowlers when I was playing, and I agree that having fresh fast bowlers coming at you all day must be tiresome. But the policy of using so much pace was effective because the other teams did not have enough good batsmen to counter it. The standard of batting has gone down. There are a few great players today, like Sunny Gavaskar, but the average Test batsman is not what he used to be.

People ask me why this is so. Why have standards dropped in cricket when runners are running faster, javelin-throwers are throwing further and high jumpers are jumping higher? The explanation is that cricket is not so much about physical fitness and reflexes. You have to be fit, of course. But to succeed you need a good technique, which must be worked at, sound concentration and courage. I have seen good players take their eye off the ball and get hit because they lacked bravery.

In the England tour of the West Indies in 1959, some of the English batsmen complained about the bowling of Chester Watson and Wes Hall, claiming it was intimidatory. But what a West Indian, brought up on hard wickets and used to the chest-high delivery, calls a bouncer and what an English player says is a bouncer are two different deliveries. A good player should be able to move behind the line of a chest-high delivery and play it down in front of him. No English player did that better than Sir Len Hutton in 1954. If he didn't want to play it, Len moved out of the line and let the ball pass.

The Englishmen were in trouble because they played sideways on, with the elbow raised in front of their face. Some of them were hit in the arm. Ken Barrington, I remember, was hit by Chester Watson on the elbow. By playing sideways on, they were unable to get their bats up high enough. If they had moved more chest-on, as I always did, their elbow would be moved to one side and they would have played the ball with the bat. Geoff Boycott suffered from this technical weakness when he first went to the West Indies. He found himself being hit on the arm a few times.

The genuine bouncer is the one that passes at head height, not chest high. It is a legitimate part of the game. In the West Indies some players will hook it for six. It is seen as an opportunity to score runs. Facing the bowlers of Clive Lloyd's team would not worry me. I would have welcomed the challenge. And so would many others, players like Seymour Nurse, Clyde Walcott, Everton Weekes, Rohan Kanhai and Conrad Hunte, all masters of the hook shot.

Are there any batsmen who are better players than these in the modern game? Viv Richards compares with them, but it is hard to think of any others playing today. Viv became a great strokemaker, a player the crowds love to watch. But for most of his career he has been an 'eye' player and has tended to play across the line occasionally. When you are young you can get away with it. Your reflexes are quick enough to get you into the right position, and you can survive the odd mistake.

Later on, the reflexes slow and the eyes are not as good. That is when the good technical player uses his experience. He can still make scores because his batting is correct. Being a great player means that when the state of the game demands a period of restraint you can do that and wrest the initiative away from the bowlers. Viv doesn't do that as often as he should: he still plays too many rash shots.

If he plays a streaky shot and gets away with it, he does not appear to think about what might happen next time if he plays the same shot. Sometimes he will play it regardless of the circumstance.

When a great batsman is at the wicket he must be controlling not only the opposing bowlers, but himself as well. As the best batsman in the side, Viv owes it to himself to play more big innings.

I do not believe the game is any more intimidatory now than it was in the past generations. In many Test matches I played in, there was no restraint on the use of short-pitched deliveries. In Australia, Dennis Lillee and Jeff Thomson didn't hold themselves back against England in 1974. Was there any more fearsome pair of opening bowlers than Dennis and Jeff? Wes and Charlie maybe, but no pair or even quartet from the modern era.

Was there any more intimidatory bowler than Harold Larwood? Sir Donald Bradman, whom I am proud to claim as a friend, has some views on that! Was there a better English bowler than Fred Trueman, a man I played against many times and admired for his tenacity, aggression and Yorkshire humour?

Far from being harder to play, I would say it is easier in some respects today. I never wore a helmet, for example. With a helmet a batsman can take more risks. I preferred to rely on my judgement and my skill with the bat. If I was somehow able to play Test cricket today, I would still not wear a helmet. They should not be part of cricket.

I was only twice struck in the head, once by a ball from a medium-pace bowler, Richard Jefferson, which I lost in the murk of the pavilion at Lord's in 1962. It knocked out two teeth, and I had eleven stitches in the mouth. After Colin Cowdrey had his arm broken in a Test match against the West Indies the following year, the MCC at last decided to install sight-screens at that end. The other occasion was in my first club match in Barbados.

Nor did I wear a thigh pad. I tried wearing one early in my career and found it cumbersome and uncomfortable. I reasoned that I had a bat to protect me. I cannot ever remember being injured by a blow on the thigh. The only protection I wore was the traditional box and pads. When I was a boy we often only had one pad between us, so we had to be sure we middled the ball!

Throughout my career I used a bat weighing two pounds four ounces. In those days that was looked upon as a fairly heavy bat.

Some of today's players use bats up to a pound heavier in weight. I think that is ludicrous. To be able to cut and hook properly, a batsman needs a lighter bat, which may be one of the reasons why so many of the modern players cannot play these shots in a competent manner.

The trend towards heavier bats was started by the South African Graeme Pollock and copied by others. If someone tries something different, there are sure to be others who will copy him. Clive Lloyd used a heavy bat and had several extra rubbers on the handle. Ian Botham is another player who likes a heavy bat. I saw one of his bats once, specially made for him by Duncan Fearnley, and was amazed to see how thick the edge was: it must have been more than an inch thick.

In my day the bowler's back foot had to be grounded behind the batting crease. That meant the fast bowler's front foot could be a yard or so beyond the popping or front crease when he released the ball. Imagine how much harder it was to score against a bowler delivering from nineteen, or less, yards away!

In 1963 the law was changed, requiring the bowler to bowl with his front foot grounded on or behind the popping crease, which had the effect of forcing him to bowl from further back. That was definitely good news for the batsman, and I think the new law has been a success. Many of the present batting records were set before the law was changed, when it was harder for the batsmen and easier for the bowlers.

It was also much easier to be caught out on the leg side when I first played. There was no restriction on fielders behind square on the leg side, and bowlers could have three, four or more fielders clustered there as in the days of Harold Larwood and leg theory. Today there is a limit of two, which usually means only one is within catching distance. I remember the Australians using the Carmody field, named after a former captain named Keith Carmody, against us - three leg slips, four slips and a gully. That would not be legal today.

There would have been more chances to have broken more records than I did if I was starting my career today. I look around and see few players of real class. Ian Botham? His name appears a the leading wicket-taker in Tests because he is a great trier and has been able to play much more cricket in a shorter period, much of it against weakened opposition, than the bowlers of the past were able to play.

Thirty years ago it was possible to play in only five Tests a year. Now it is anything up to twelve. It is now far easier to break records. Fred Trueman's 67 Tests occupied fifteen years, and he took 307 wickets. Botham's Test career was in its tenth year, in which time he took part in 85 tests, when he beat Dennis Lillee's record of 355 against New Zealand in 1986.

I judge greatness on the quality of the opposition. Would Botham have taken so many wickets if he was playing regularly against Weekes, Worrell, Walcott and the other great players of my time? I doubt it. When he toured the West Indies in 1985–6 Ian took 11 wickets at 48 apiece. Eventually he should pass 400 wickets and may end up the leading wicket-taker in the history of Tests. That would still not make him the greatest bowler.

Ian could have stamped himself as one of the greatest all-rounders very early in his career if his batting had been more responsible. He wanted to play his shots too early. You cannot slog good bowling, particularly the West Indian bowling. Even the best players have to graft and build an innings.

Keith Miller was a better all-rounder than Ian Botham because he had more style. He was a faster, more threatening bowler.

I have already shown that figures cannot be a true guide to making comparisons between players of different eras, but Miller had the advantage both with the bat (his average was 36 against Botham's 35) and with the ball (170 wickets at twenty-two against Botham's 373 at twenty-eight at the end of the 1987 Pakistan series in England). In Miller's day Australia played matches only against the senior Test-match-playing countries: England, West Indies, India and South Africa.

Botham's bowling record could be overtaken by Richard Hadlee, a thinking bowler who must be rated a great all-rounder in any company. He is the one I most admire of the present all-rounders.

He has taken wickets against the best batsmen on their own pitches. He's proved himself.

Pakistan's Imran Khan has impressive figures and is a fine cricketer, but only became a Test-class batsman in the last five years of his career. He can now build an innings in the interests of his side. He has achieved that by hard work and much practice. With the ball, Imran has a high strike rate against the best players, and he is such an inspirational figure as captain that when he had a fractured shin and was out of Test cricket for a long time Pakistan's results slumped. When he was fit and returned, Pakistan once again became one of the best sides in the world. They managed to beat England on their own pitches for the first time.

Imran is one of the group of twenty-two Test players who scored more than 1000 runs and took more than 100 wickets in their Test career. Botham, Kapil Dev and Hadlee are the other ones from the modern game. Kapil has a high strike rate of wickets, but I suspect he may not play much longer. He reached the target in 25 Tests against the 23 Tests of his predecessor in the Indian side, Vinoo Mankad.

Vinoo was one of the slowest bowlers I played against in Tests. He would be a test for many of today's batsmen, who rarely have to bat against bowlers of his type. We faced back-of-the-hand bowlers like Jack Walsh, George Tribe, Jack Hill and Lindsay Kline – bowlers who spun the ball a lot. There are no bowlers of that type today to worry anyone.

In my day the administrators ruled cricket. Today much of the power rests with the players. They decide whether they will go on tours. Politics has intruded, and there is more animosity. I can see no solution to that. If governments give money to a sport, they want to have a say in how it is run. As a cricketer, I wanted to play with anyone who wanted to play against me. There should be no barriers.

People ask me if I would like to face all that fast bowling today. I would not be unhappy about it. I learned not to duck in 1954 when I was playing against Fred Trueman. Freddie bowled a short one and

I ducked, only to find it didn't bounce as much as I expected. I had to go so slow that I actually hit my forehead on the bat.

The only other time I ducked was in Australia several years later when I was playing for South Australia and Wes Hall was playing for Queensland.

On this occasion I had made only a handful of runs when Wes, fielding in the unaccustomed position of slip, dropped a snick off me. He usually fielded on the boundary. The miss rankled him, and he started to run in very quick and let a few short balls fly at me. Later on, I moved into the nineties by hooking him for six. I knew when Wes was about to bowl a bouncer because his stride would shorten as he approached the crease.

He came in again, and I could see it was to be another bouncer, so I ducked. That made him much happier.

'I made you duck, you bitch,' he said.

'I did it to help you, man,' I said. 'You been having a hard time of it!'

In the West Indies we try to play the game attractively and provide excitement for the spectators. That was the way I tried to play, whether it was bowling, batting or fielding. In England they seem too bothered about over rates. If the game is being deliberately slowed down by the fielding side, as has happened on a number of occasions, particularly involving English teams, then I say there is reason for concern.

But if a team has a number of fast bowlers with long run-ups the over rate will be slower. The important thing is whether the cricket is stimulating. Are there shots being played? Wickets knocked over? Great catches being made? If the West Indies over rate had been speeded up during the 'blackwash' series in England in 1984, some of the matches would have been over in two or three days. Would the administrators want that?

Cricket is a game to be enjoyed, and I enjoyed my twenty years at the top. If I hadn't, I would have got out and concentrated on golf (my handicap at the moment is 3 and not likely to improve). I could never have been a grafter, a player forsaking all risks.

My batting was based on watching the many good, and some

great players in Barbados. I saw how they did things and came home and practised them for myself. I was never coached. I liked to improvise but I did not go in for some of the fancy shots today's batsmen use, like the reverse sweep.

I think that shot is nonsensical. It gives the bowler too much of a chance. Mushtaq was the first batsman I saw use it. One-day cricket has made batsmen think of new ways to beat defensive bowling and well-set fields. I approved of Kerry Packer's World Series Cricket in Australia because it upgraded the status of cricketers and made them better-paid. It broadened cricket's appeal. The use of coloured clothing attracted women spectators. There are more women than ever watching cricket these days.

Yet I believe there is now too much one-day cricket being played, particularly in Australia. One-day cricket is popular and brings in finance which is essential because the game has never been really profitable. The cost of taking teams around the world for long periods is too high.

But it doesn't breed good cricketers: it can ruin them instead. The breeding-grounds for Test players are the club sides and the county and state sides where three- and four-day cricket is played which gives young batsmen the opportunity to build an innings.

When young players have to go in and score quickly from the start, which is usually the way on one-day matches, they are forced to take chances. They play technically bad shots like the 'steer' through the vacant slip positions.

Shoving youngsters into that environment is like asking a baby to run before he can crawl. My solution would be to leave the younger, inexperienced players out of one-day games. Let them have four or five years' experience in normal cricket where they can learn their trade. One-day cricket should be for players who have had an apprenticeship, players whose technique won't be ruined by one-day cricket.

I retired before one-day cricket got the hold it has today but I would have played exactly the same way, using the same methods. England has the right idea. It has limited the number of one-day internationals to three against a visiting touring side. When there is a one-day international almost weekly, as can happen in Australia, it devalues the game.

I also recommend the selection of two different teams – one to play the one-day matches and the other to take part in five-day Tests. There will be players who are good enough to compete in both one-day and five-day cricket – the Bothams, Hadlees and Marshalls. But there are others who are one-day specialists. They will never be five-day cricketers because they do not have the necessary concentration and patience.

One-day cricket is becoming more popular throughout the world, even in India where Test matches were nearly always attended by huge crowds. Now attendances there are falling. People want to see the excitement of one-day cricket.

Will one-day cricket swamp Test cricket and destroy it? I do not think so. There are enough far-sighted people in the game to prevent that happening. But it must be kept in check. Test cricket is the highest form of cricket, showing off every aspect of the game and not just a certain number. It must survive.

I have said that batting standards have fallen, and I believe that bowling standards have also slipped. One-day cricket must share some of the blame for that. In limited-overs cricket the aim of the bowlers is to contain, to stop the batsmen making a big score. If a bowler takes 0–20 in ten overs, he has done a fine job. The slower bowlers like John Emburey and Eddie Hemmings, who were both successful in the fourth World Cup, push the ball through flatter and restrict the range of shots open to the batsman.

That works in one-day cricket, but it won't get people out in five-day cricket. On good batting pitches, spinners have to flight the ball and vary their pace and amount of turn. Bowling is a craft in Test cricket. Similarly with quicker bowlers, who have to work out different attacking methods of getting batsmen out as opposed to merely containing them.

Learning any profession requires hard work, and I think I did enough of that in my younger days. I was always in the nets working on my game. Some people may have thought I was a lucky cricketer because I went for my shots and sometimes got away with a streaky shot. It reminded me of the comment of the South African golfer Gary Player. 'Lucky?' he said. 'The more I practise, the luckier I get!'

I was born with five fingers on each hand, and babies with extra fingers are supposed to be born lucky. I had one removed when I was at school but played for a year or two with the other before it was cut off.

One thing worries me about cricket as the game approaches its third century since it began in England: not so many boys are interested in taking it up. Not just cricket, but other sports as well. My sons have so many other things to occupy their minds – television, videos, surfboards and many other distractions. Many potential young cricketers will be lost to the game, and there may not be enough sufficiently dedicated to do what I did – come from the backstreets to reach the top in the game.

My brothers and I used to play cricket almost every waking hour. If not cricket, then football, or table tennis or basketball. We were mad on sport. In those days the sporting heroes like Sir Stanley Matthews in football, the 'three Ws' in cricket, and Fred Perry in tennis did not make fortunes and retire millionaires like some of the sportsmen today. They played sport because they loved it. In the West Indies, our motivation was to travel. If we could reach a certain standard in cricket, we could get a job with a League club in England or represent our country on tours abroad.

Today the incentive is money, plenty of it. But not many boys want to take up sport. I find that very strange. But the more dedicated ardent sports-lovers will come through.

2 | Captaining a Winning Side

As a captain, I always believed that it was worth taking a chance to win and keep interest alive. I tried to give the other side a chance of victory. I did not believe in batting on so long that the other team would be forced to bat defensively. If a team is concentrating exclusively on trying to survive, that makes for boring cricket.

I discovered that too many rival captains were frightened of taking the slightest chance because they feared losing and being criticised. That never worried me. I did what I thought was right for cricket, and for the spectators who pay money to watch. The game is more important than winning or losing. Cricketers are entertainers. If they bore people, they are killing their own profession.

The time when my judgement over a declaration attracted the strongest criticism was during the Fourth Test against England in Port of Spain in March 1968. The England side was captained by Colin Cowdrey, whom I liked immensely as a person. But you could never call Colin an adventurous captain. Brian Close was the first choice of the selectors, but the MCC ruled him out after his censure for time-wasting in a county game.

The first three matches had been drawn and, though we nearly won the Second Test after a bottle-throwing incident when England were holding on at 68–8, the series had not been a memorable one. Some magnificent batting in Port of Spain by Seymour Nurse (136) and Rohan Kanhai (153) enabled me to declare at 526–7. England's first innings was meandering along with Cowdrey in the runs when I had the inspiration to try Basil Butcher's flighted leg-breaks. Basil ended Cowdrey's innings on 148 with a decision which the England players did not like and proceeded to take 5–15 in ten overs.

Alan Knott, an excellent player of spin bowling, finished on 69 not out. Knotty was a marvellous sweeper of the ball, and his judgement was unerring. The West Indies had a lead of 122, and had made 92–2 in the second innings when I decided to declare. I cannot recall too many experts saying at the time that it was a foolhardy declaration. England were asked to score 215 in two and three-quarter hours, or 78 runs an hour. They had never got anywhere near that rate previously in the series.

The West Indies had no fast bowlers other than myself, because Wes Hall had been dropped and Charlie Griffith pulled a muscle early in England's first innings. Charlie had a run-out in the nets on the Monday morning, but it was felt he couldn't bowl in a match. I opened the bowling myself with Lance Gibbs. It was the final day, and the Queen's Park pitch traditionally took more turn the longer the game went on. The other bowlers available to me were Joey Carew, Basil Butcher and Willie Rodriguez.

On his home pitch, Willie was often a match-winner. He bowled leg-breaks and googlies at a fair pace and, though occasionally erratic, could bowl deliveries which were almost unplayable.

In my first over Deryck Murray, normally a good catcher to the quicker bowlers, dropped John Edrich who went on to help Geoff Boycott put on 55 in the first 19 overs. In the many inquests afterwards, I did not hear anyone mention that incident. If Edrich had gone then, I am reasonably confident England would not have gone for the runs. Cowdrey and Boycott went serenely on, and it did not appear to me that England were interested in accepting my challenge. The game would have petered out in a boring draw if I had not declared. Now it was doing so despite the declaration.

Several England players revealed in the books written later that some strong words were said at the interval. Ken Barrington and Basil d'Oliveira in particular felt Cowdrey and Boycott should go for the target. They were backed by Tom Graveney. After tea, Cowdrey and Boycott accelerated the run rate. When I caught Cowdrey for 71 off Lance Gibbs it was nearly all over. Basil Butcher could not repeat his success of the first innings, and Willie Rodriguez was hit for 35 in 10 overs after bowling Edrich for 29.

England won with three minutes to spare, with Boycott 80 not out. The West Indies bowling rate was 19 an hour, which contrasted with the 22 bowled in two hours by England's bowlers in the morning when they were trying to slow the game down. It did not occur to me to slow the game down. That was not my style of playing cricket. I was trying to win the match, not draw it. England's victory gave them the Wisden Trophy, which was being played for by the two countries for the first time.

I was left to regret an incident the previous August in Barbados when a pedestrian walked out into the road in front of Wes Hall's car, causing the vehicle to swerve off the road. The pedestrian wasn't hurt – he jumped back to safety – but Wes damaged a knee and wasn't fully fit during the series when he took only 9 wickets at 39 each.

When a captain wins, he is applauded and hailed as a great captain. When he loses, he is a fool and deserves to be sacked. There were many people calling for my removal after that match! It was one of 10 Tests I lost in the 39 I captained the West Indies. For several years we were the best team in the world. I do not think my record was a bad one.

The best West Indian captain was, in my opinion, the late Sir Frank Worrell. Sir Frank was the first captain to bring the players of the countries of the Caribbean together and mould them into a team, every man playing for the team and not for himself. There were no cliques. He would not allow them. Sir Frank achieved this unity in Australia in 1960–1.

I learned a lot from Sir Frank. He was good at talking to bowlers in such a way that they did not feel they were being criticised. He would make suggestions to them about where they should be bowling. He would do it with a joke or a smile. He was in command but he was not an authoritarian captain. I tried to be the same. He recognised that some players – and I was one – couldn't sleep if they went to bed early, so he did not discourage them from having a drink. But if they did drink and came in late, and it affected their performance, he would show his displeasure. It wouldn't happen again.

The prime asset of a captain is being able to read the game and have a deep knowledge of it. If he qualifies on that score, he earns the respect of his players. He must, of course, be good enough to hold a place in the side on his playing ability. There have been examples where a player's right to a place has been questionable – England's Mike Brearley was an example.

The captain must be a good leader. He must know which player to scold and which one to encourage. He must involve the other players, listening to them when they offer advice. Sometimes it will be nonsense. Other times a senior player will have made a good point which will benefit the side.

Team meetings at which tactics are discussed have long been a feature of Test cricket. The captain will work out a strategy with his players. The bowlers will talk about how they want to bowl and what fields they will require. When the West Indies played against England we would plan to try to dismiss Geoff Boycott as quickly as possible because we saw him as the anchor man of the side, the one we had to get out to make the rest of the batting shaky.

If Boycott was vulnerable to anything, it was to the in-swinging delivery bowled by a fast left-hand bowler. That was why I would often put myself on to bowl against him. Once he was set, it was not easy to dismiss Geoffrey. You could wait a long time for him to make a mistake.

No captain can work out all his plans in advance. He has to see the state of the pitch first and assess the effect of the weather. I enjoyed my time as captain because it meant I was involved in the game the whole time. I used to speak to my players constantly, encouraging them wherever possible and making points which I felt could benefit both them and the team.

In the sixties the West Indies had a balanced attack, and I had to consider when to bring the spin bowlers on and from which end. This is not meant as a criticism, but I believe Clive Lloyd, who captained the West Indies in 79 Tests and was the most successful of them all in terms of matches won, did not have to make as many decisions as I did. When his team was in its prime, he had four outstanding fast bowlers whom he used in spells. He rarely had to wonder when to change the formula and bring on a spinner.

But Clive should be given the credit for deciding to go into a Test match with four fast bowlers. Douglas Jardine was the first to try it, in the Bodyline series in Australia in 1932–3. He did it for a specific purpose – to stop Don Bradman making a colossal number of runs.

Sir Len Hutton tried it once in Australia with disastrous results, losing a Test in Brisbane by a record number of runs. Lloyd first adopted the idea in the Second Test in Melbourne in 1975–6, his third series in charge, and his pace bowlers were Andy Roberts, Keith Boyce, Michael Holding and Bernard Julien. West Indies won that match easily to square the series at 1–1, and after his success in the 1975 Prudential World Cup and also in a series in India Lloyd must have been anticipating another triumph.

Holding missed the next Test in Melbourne through injury, and Lloyd's side collapsed, losing the series 5–1 with Jeff Thomson taking 29 wickets and Dennis Lillee 27. It was a jolting moment for Lloyd and West Indies cricket. But he managed to pull the team round, mould it together and start winning again.

When I was captain the chief motivation for the players was the opportunity to play for their country and travel the world. Not all were full-time professionals, and many of them had jobs outside cricket. If I tried to make too many demands, they would say: 'Hey, I've got a job to go back to. I'm not doing this for my living.'

After the intervention of Kerry Packer's World Series Cricket, the West Indies Board was forced to pay the players enough money to make them full-time cricketers. The motivation was now money, and plenty of it. That made Lloyd's task easier. The big prizes were driving the players to greater efforts and were helping to mould a better team spirit. There was no problem getting bowlers to bowl flat out, or batsmen to play an innings. Almost overnight, the West Indies side became a very professional team. An Australian, Dennis Waight, was appointed to take the physical training, and the players became fitter than any other West Indies side.

With constant daily practice the standard of catching improved enormously. If I had to give a reason why the West Indies once again became the best team in the world, I would say it was because of the high percentage of catches being held as much as the quality of the fast bowling.

The squad of fast bowlers, Roberts, Holding and Garner later augmented by Croft and Marshall, were tremendous bowlers. You could stick an ordinary bowler among that lot and he would find himself taking a lot of wickets. And they were backed by great catching.

Opposing batsmen were in a bad state when they knew they had to face this calibre of bowling not just in the first few hours of play but all day and every day they batted. Batsmen who might have been confident about scoring runs became less confident. Some panicked. The calypso kings sang: 'If Holding and Roberts don't get you, Marshall or Garner must.'

Viv Richards, so long in the shadow of Lloyd, had a difficult task when he took over in 1985 because Roberts had gone, Holding was no longer as fast, Croft had long since departed, and Garner was on the verge of quitting. Only Marshall was the same. The saying that a captain is only as good as his players is a true one, and with the fast bowlers no longer available in most cases and the younger ones not yet ready Viv knew he had a job to do. In the Reliance World Cup one of his leading batsmen, Gordon Greenidge, was not available and nor was his best bowler, Marshall. In those circumstances, any side would struggle, whoever was in charge. I do not know of many instances, if any, where a good captain made a poor side into a winning side.

I thought Richards made a good start. His team beat England 5–0 in the West Indies, drew 1–1 in Pakistan – a hard place to achieve victory – beat New Zealand at home and drew away. All presentable results.

I do not know enough about what happens inside the dressing room to discuss Viv's style of captaincy. I myself suffered from critics who did not know much of what was going on, so I will not make that mistake. But he needs to follow Clive Lloyd's example with the bat to consolidate his position. Clive became a much more reliable player when he was made captain. He was the player the others all expected to make runs, whatever the state of the game. And he usually made them. He commanded their respect both as a captain and as a player.

Viv has to do that. He has to bat more responsibly and not expect nearly every ball to be hit to the boundary. He has to look on himself as the mainstay of the innings. He must set an example to the other, younger batsmen. I do not see many good young prospects appearing in Shell Shield cricket who could become as good as the players who have left. There are many fast bowlers around but none good enough.

Experienced fast bowlers who might have helped out until the next generation emerges – Ezra Moseley, Franklyn Stephenson and Sylvester Clarke – are all banned from international cricket after going on a representative tour to South Africa. All three of them would strengthen the current West Indies side. And they all have experience of playing in England. I would class Sylvester as the quickest and most hostile fast bowler now playing in world cricket, more hostile even than Malcolm Marshall. He is capable of getting the ball to rise to chest height from a length.

A few years ago I was taking part in a floodlit game at the National Stadium, and most of the best bowlers from Barbados were playing. The pitch was a strip of Astroturf stretched across the centre of the football ground.

Sylvester came on to bowl, and the ball came through like a shot from a gun.

'You can't bowl like that,' I said. 'You'll kill someone.'

'Skipper,' he replied, 'if you don't want me to bowl, then take me off. I don't know any other way to bowl.'

Rohan Kanhai was playing in that match. Rohan was my successor as West Indian captain, and I would not fault him. He had a good cricket brain and earned the respect of his players. As a player, Rohan could allow himself to be riled occasionally by players who deliberately set out to disturb his concentration. He was famous for that sweep shot of his when he used to fall over.

People thought he was lucky to hit the ball for sixes, but it was done intentionally. Rohan knew what he was doing.

He was an outstanding hooker, though he didn't relish being bounced. Bowlers would be making a huge mistake if they said to him: 'I'm going to knock you down.' When that happened, he would be more determined to hit them out of the ground. He had his pride.

The best English captain of my time was Brian Close. Brian played cricket like a West Indian: he was always on the attack, always looking for ways to win a game. He would never set the field back. And he never worried about the reputation of his opponents.

An example of his fearless approach was the way he got me out at the Oval in 1966. I came in at 74–4 to partner Rohan, who went on to make 104, and Close stationed himself a yard or two from the bat at short leg. He was not wearing a helmet – no one did in those days – nor any other form of protection. Afterwards I learned he had told John Snow to bowl a bouncer.

Snow sent down a poor attempt at a bouncer. It was more like a long hop. I swung round to despatch it to the boundary but tried to hit the ball so hard that I played too soon. It came off the bottom of the bat, bounced off my thigh and lobbed into the hands of Close.

A child of ten could have caught it, but no other player in the game would have been standing up like that. Once he saw me going for the pull shot, any other fielder would have taken evasive action. Brian Close did not believe in that. I never saw him flinch. Ten years later, at the age of forty-five, he was still standing up to the world's fastest bowlers when he made a comeback against the West Indies and Andy Roberts, Michael Holding and Wayne Daniel gave him a peppering at Old Trafford. It was a repeat of his performance against us at Lord's in 1963 when he let some deliveries from Wes Hall and Charlie Griffith hit him in the body rather than play a risky shot.

I never met a braver player than Brian. If he was hit, he didn't show any pain. He just got on with it. As a batsman, he knew his limitations. I would rather have a gutsy player like him in my side than a more gifted player who lacked courage. Mike Gatting, the present England captain, has some of Close's qualities when it comes to standing up to fast bowling. He, too, is a brave player.

Whether it was for Yorkshire, Somerset or England, I never failed to have an enjoyable game with Close when he was skipper. He always tried to keep the interest going and get a result. If a game was dying, I would lose interest, my motivation would go. I believe he was the same.

He should have played more for England than he did: 22 Tests was not a fair reflection of his contribution to English cricket. The authorities never forgave him for the time-wasting affair at Edgbaston in 1967 just prior to the series in the West Indies when he was lined up to captain England. He was not the first English captain to waste time!

Most English captains tend to be too conservative – Len Hutton, Peter May, Colin Cowdrey, Mike Smith, Mike Denness, Ray Illingworth and Bob Willis among them. Their first priority is to avoid defeat. Once they reach that target and they start getting on top, they begin to attack.

Illingworth, whom I liked, had a sound Yorkshire apprenticeship and was a keen student of the game. But he was typically English in his style of leadership, unwilling to take chances and only committing himself when the odds were in his favour.

He knew when he had the upper hand and did his best to exploit the situation. He would let you make mistakes and then pounce. He would not risk making one himself. So many English captains were like that: they would sit back, keep it tight and hope the opposition slipped up somewhere. They did not make any positive moves which might fail.

Against the West Indies, Illy tried to tie our batsmen down and frustrate them. It didn't succeed, and he lost his job like a football manager with a losing team.

Ted Dexter was much criticised when he led England, but I thought he was one of the better England captains. He was prepared to gamble and did not have the same defensive philosophy of his contemporaries. I thought he was a tremendous person, and we got on extremely well – especially on the golf-course.

Ted was a perfectionist. He was always talking to himself when he batted. 'Come on, Ted,' he used to say. And he would practise his shots as though he felt something needed sorting out in his game.

He was the same at golf. I played with him at Wentworth once, and he went round in 68. There was little doubt that he could have become a top golfer. Instead of being delighted, he was dissatisfied about one particular shot and went back outside and paid for a lesson to sort out the problem. He was very competitive and wanted to win all the time.

His chief weakness was that he would come up with a theory and stick with it whatever was happening in the game. Or he would have another, more promising theory, which he would talk himself out of and then try something different.

As a batsman I rated him in the very highest class, ahead of May and Cowdrey. He had the great player's ability to make the good ball look a bad one. He didn't respect any bowler. His 70 off 73 deliveries at Lord's in 1963, one of the finest 'non-hundreds' of that Test series, showed the qualities which made him one of the greatest players England has ever produced.

He came in at 2–1 with Wes Hall and Charlie Griffith bowling at their fastest. Both bowlers were in their prime, and Frank Worrell kept them going for long spells. Most batsmen would have taken a look at the situation and tried to play themselves in quietly. But Ted started driving Wes and Charlie straight with shots which rang out around the packed ground like pistol shots. I remember one straight drive off Charlie which went so fast that Charlie only just managed to lift his boot out of the way before it was bouncing back off the pavilion wall.

Next ball Charlie slipped in the short one. Ted swivelled round and clipped it through mid-wicket for another boundary. He was in full command. I admired his style and his stroke-play. Frank Worrell asked me to bowl at the pavilion end, and I had Ted lbw with the inswinger. That wicket gave me immense pleasure. I particularly enjoyed getting great players out when they were in full flow.

Ted concentrated much harder than most players, which was one of the secrets of his success. It is a mistake for a batsman to stand up after the ball has been bowled and watch the bowler walk back to his mark. He will probably be thinking about what to expect next. Will it be a bouncer? Or a yorker? Anxiety will build up, tiring him out mentally as well as physically. I used to pat the pitch with my bat and look all around the ground – anywhere except at the bowler until he was ready to bowl. My mind would be on something else.

Hanif Mohammad was one of the best players at concentrating at the crease, which was just as well since he seemed to spend a large part of his career batting. He used to take a couple of steps down the pitch and twirl his bat around before pretending to pat the pitch.

Geoff Boycott was another who relied on concentration and application. He always felt he should have captained England on more occasions, but because of his single-mindedness he was too selfish a player. A captain has to be constantly thinking of the players under him. Once I was playing for Nottinghamshire against him, and the Yorkshire players were upset at the way he ran a couple of them out. Later we chatted, and he said: 'You and I are the best two players in the world and, if I'm batting, the other batsman must be willing to run himself out for me.' I said I could not agree. There were occasions when a tail-ender might have to sacrifice himself, but to run out an accredited batsman was not right. 'If senior batsmen had run you out earlier in your career, you wouldn't have become a great player,' I said. My approach was the opposite to Boycott's. I was never worried about getting out. If quick runs were needed, no matter whether I was in the nineties or not, I would try to get them. At Trent Bridge in 1966 the West Indies had to score quickly on the Monday, and I was caught at 94 going for a big hit off Ken Higgs. If I was greedy, I could have pushed for a century.

England had three captains in the 1966 series and only the last one, Brian Close, showed the necessary qualities to put us under any threat. Mike Smith, who led in the First Test, was typically English in his approach, very cautious, and Colin Cowdrey was little better.

Peter May, who led England against the West Indies in 1957 and for the first three Tests in 1959–60 before becoming ill and handing over to Cowdrey, was also a restrained and unadventurous captain.

As a player, Peter played mainly off the front foot, and as a result was limited against the bouncer. Good bouncers always had him in trouble. If he was starting his career today, I think he would be a worried man.

I have never objected to the bowler's right to bowl bouncers. In the West Indies and India in particular the pitches are so flat that the odds are all in favour of the batsman. All the law changes made in cricket to my knowledge have favoured batsmen and penalised bowlers – the front-foot law, leg-side limitation on fielders, intimidatory bowling and no lbw to a delivery pitched outside the leg stump. The bouncer is the one legal weapon left to the bowler.

Used properly, it can upset the concentration of a batsman and make him apprehensive. If the batsman is a good hooker, it is a bad ball because it will cost runs. The bowler has to know how to ration it. Some couldn't do that, and I remember a former West Indies fast bowler, Uton Dowe from Jamaica, continuing to send down bouncers when he was being punished by the Australians in 1973. The crowd became so fed up with him that they stuck up a banner which said: 'Dowe shalt not bowl.'

The bowler ought to have the cricketing intelligence to know when he is over-using the bouncer. If he overdoes it, it no longer has the element of surprise.

I believe there is an obsession about bouncers in England. The commentators and administrators talk so much about short-pitched bowling that there is always a demand to do something about it. They have an experimental law of only one per over, which is nonsense really. When Joel Garner used to get the ball up from just short of a length on a hard bouncy pitch, was that considered a bouncer? My definition of a good bouncer is a short ball which comes through head high.

Law 42 is adequate as it stands: that if the umpire feels a bowler is bowling short so that injury might be inflicted on the batsman he can call 'No ball' and warn the bowler. The trouble is that there is so much pressure coming from those outside the field of play that umpires often take action when none is needed.

Batsmen, too, have to use their brains. Several West Indian

batsmen were caught hooking bouncers in Australia in 1975–6 because the boundaries were so large in Melbourne. Peter May was not the only batsman labelled 'great' who failed against the bouncer. Australia's Greg Chappell was another. The West Indies used to have him caught off top-edged hook shots regularly, and he still went on playing them.

Tony Greig was a different type. He was a talking captain, a man who tried to intimidate his opponents. If he said he was going to do something, he did it.

When he made his 'I'll make them grovel' statement on television, it upset the West Indian players and they took an added delight in taking his wicket. Knowing Greig, I am sure he relished the extra challenge his interview provoked. He was a good communicator, with his players, the crowd and the press. He upset the cricketing authorities with the way he recruited the world's best players to take part in World Series Cricket, but I do not believe he could have done it any other way.

Mike Brearley enjoys a good reputation as a successful England captain, but it was based on three winning series at a time when Australian and Pakistani cricket was ravaged by World Series Cricket, and much of that success was gained by the exploits of Ian Botham.

He led England to victory against Pakistan in 1978 when their best players had gone to World Series Cricket in Australia, and he was also victorious in series against New Zealand and India. At no time did he lead England against the strongest team of the age, the West Indies. I believe he came along at an opportune time.

My assessment of greatness in cricket, whether it is in batting, bowling, fielding or captaincy, is that the claimant competes with the best in that field and proves his ability. I do not accept that Brearley qualifies. He missed out on the contests for the world championship by not playing against the West Indies. Nor did I rate him as a Test-class batsman. He was an ordinary player.

Ian Botham skippered England in the two series against the West Indies in 1980 and 1981, and it came too soon for him. He was too young, too inexperienced. I do not think he is suitable for captaincy anyway. He is too aggressive. A good captain has to be a diplomat and has to set a good example. Botham took too many chances as a batsman. How could he reprimand a player for throwing his wicket away when he did it himself? His type of player performs better if he has someone he respects guiding his career. If Brearley had a major achievement to his credit, it was getting the best out of Ian Botham.

David Gower's reign showed the truth of the statement that a captain is no better or no worse than his players. Gower's players did not perform against the West Indies. They were over-awed. Ian Botham seemed to be able to do what he liked, bowling too long and coming on when it might have been beneficial to try another bowler.

David had long been looked on as a coming England captain, a very good player but not yet a great player, a man who commanded respect. But it didn't work out for him. Mike Gatting is much firmer, a seemingly stronger personality who can handle temperamental players. Mike gets more out of the players, is more outgoing and more flexible. When he is in the field, he gives the appearance of being in charge. And he has tremendous guts as a batsman.

He is the nearest captain in outlook to Brian Close, though not as bold. Now England have a manager in Micky Stewart they are a more professional side and in a better position to avenge the heavy defeats suffered at the hands of the West Indies. The idea of appointing a full-time manager who is also the coach is a good one. There is more need for such a manager than when I was playing and the players were less professional.

He can improve discipline because, unlike the captain, he does not have to coax greater effort from the players on the field. As he is so close to them, the captain sometimes has to make concessions. The manager can be much firmer. The players will have to trust him and respect his record as a Test player. If he has not played many Tests and has been largely unsuccessful, he will not win over the younger players.

If the West Indies decide to appoint a full-time manager, the prime candidate will surely be Clive Lloyd if he is interested in the post. Should Wes Hall be available, he would be ideal, but Wes is too busy as a government minister in Barbados.

Australia has had one of its finest captains, Bobby Simpson, as cricket manager and, though Bobby has an astute cricket brain, the experiment was not as successful as in England until Allan Border's team surprised everyone by winning the Reliance World Cup. Australia, with Allan Border as captain and Simpson as manager, twice lost to New Zealand. They couldn't cope with the bowling of Richard Hadlee. Richard has mastered his art and uses all his weapons at the right time. Great players, whether batsmen or bowlers, are always in control. Hadlee is always controlling any situation he is in.

The outstanding Australian captain in my time was Ian Chappell. He was vastly superior to his brother Greg as a leader, and I think he was also a better batsman. Ian probably had the support of his players more than any captain with the possible exception of Sir Frank Worrell. He would do anything for them, and they would do anything for him.

He was a hard competitor and would try to disturb the concentration of opponents by his words and actions. Tony Lock and Tony Greig used to do that, and it never worried me. I knew what they were going to do. It would spur me on. What may have been an insult to one person may not be an insult to another. I have never talked to opponents in that way myself – it is called 'sledging' in Australia – nor would I allow my players to use those tactics.

I only played against Richie Benaud in one series as captain, in 1960–1, but he struck me as being a fine captain, shrewd and understanding and having the wholehearted support of the men under him. Bobby Simpson, who followed him was always a tough competitor who played it fairly. His batting partner Bill Lawry was in charge in 1968–9 when, because of 34 dropped catches, we lost the series 3–1, and I found his captaincy as mean as his batting. He gave you the time of day but little else.

Probably the best New Zealand captain I knew was Geoff Howarth. And the most gentlemanly was Graham Dowling, now secretary of the Board. The Nawab of Pataudi was a good leader of the Indian side I skippered against in 1966–7; and Ajit Wadekar, who led the Indians against us in 1970–1, was the sharpest.

Before the start of play in the Fifth Test in Port of Spain I walked out to the middle with Ajit, accompanied by the usual group of groundstaff, officials and others. I threw the coin up, Ajit called, and I was sure I had won. I said I would go back to the dressing-room and talk to the players before making a decision. The Indians led 1–0, and we needed to win the last Test to square the series.

Once inside the dressing-room, I was amazed to hear a loudspeaker announcement saying that India had won the toss and would bat. One of the locals stuck his head into the room and said: 'What's going on? You won it, didn't you?' I didn't think it was worth arguing. There were no independent witnesses. Everyone else out in the middle had been a West Indian. I asked Wadekar about it later, and he failed to reply.

Despite suffering from toothache, Sunny Gavaskar scored 124 and 220 in that match and we lost the rubber. He showed in that first Test series what a wonderful player he was, and eighteen years later he was still scoring runs against the world's best bowlers. He's a man who has proved his greatness. And he wasn't a bad captain, either.

3 | Playing It My Way

Some critics used to say I was an instinctive player but I think I should be given credit for natural ability. It is what you do with it that counts. I worked hard at improving my game in the nets.

Some players go to the nets to try to see how far they can hit the ball. They do not take their practice seriously. I believe Ian Botham is such a player. But how much better a player would he have been had he worked at his game? No one knows, but he may well have broken some batting records along the way.

I do not know where my natural ability came from or who gave it to me. Perhaps only God knows that. My father played football and a little cricket. My athleticism and agility may have been hereditary. I do not know. My father died when I was five, and I never discussed it with my mother.

But from an early age I thought about my game and what I should do to improve myself as a cricketer. I was never coached, which may not have been a handicap. Some coaches tell you wrong things. For instance, some will tell a young batsman to go down the pitch to slow bowlers to hit them off their length. I figured that there are enough ways for a bowler to get you out – why give him another one? So I never went down the pitch to hit slow bowlers. In my 130 Test innings, I was only stumped once. I believe that was the only time I was ever stumped, in my career. If the bowler was dropping it short enough to entice the batsman to go out, why not wait for it and hit the ball off the back foot? That is what I used to do. It gave me longer to look at the ball to see what it was doing.

I can only recall one occasion when I charged recklessly down the pitch. It was while playing for my club side in Barbados, Police, against Harrison College. The College had a slow leg-break and googly bowler named Eddie Perkins. He used to throw the ball up into the air and turn it a lot. I misread his googly, missed my shot and turned to see what I thought would be an inevitable stumping. But the wicket-keeper, Albert Hassell, misread the googly as well and the ball went for byes. Next Saturday I scored 202, and the fielding side were most unhappy with Albert!

After that, I reasoned that the crease belongs to the batsman. Why give it up? In the nets I used to work out where I would hit the ball, how I would play certain shots. When I played in a match, I would use that knowledge to find the gaps in the field.

Another idea I had was to stand six inches to a foot outside the crease to the fast bowlers which obviously meant the ball was coming on to me that much quicker. Batsmen usually prefer to stand further away from the genuine fast bowlers, not closer to them!

I did it only when the fast bowlers were bowling to me and the wicket-keeper was standing back. By being out of my ground, I forced the bowler to drop the ball a little shorter. I was able to reach the ball on the front foot if I wanted to and also take a big step back to play a shot on the back foot. When you are standing in the crease the proximity of the stumps limits the distance you can step back. Also, it minimised my chances of being lbw. I always did this when facing fast bowlers, and it usually proved successful.

Another idea I had enabled me to take many catches I would never otherwise have reached. It was to stand no more than a yard from the bat at backward short leg when Lance Gibbs or any other off-break bowler was bowling. I reasoned that if the ball was pitched straight, and the batsman was merely attempting to play it down in front of him, I could take another step forward and catch it before it hit the ground. I took a number of chances off Lance in this way.

I always watched the line of the ball when the bowler delivered it. If the line was outside the leg stump and the batsman started to pick up his bat to bring it across for the sweep shot, I moved to a safe position behind the wicket-keeper.

There was one occasion when I didn't move quickly enough. It was in Australia, and the batsman was Ian Chappell. Ian took me unawares by sweeping a ball from David Holford pitched outside the off stump. It struck me on the chest before I could take evasive action. Fortunately I clutched it to my chest and, though it was very painful, I was delighted to have got rid of such a dangerous batsman.

All cricketers need luck, especially young ones, and though I was dropped on many occasions by fielders I always maintained I was not a lucky cricketer. When I hit the ball in the air, it tended to go towards a fielder and would stick.

Young players need luck, because their concentration isn't as good as that of older players and they take unnecessary risks. During my first tour of England in 1957, several of the senior players said I should get a lot more runs in Tests than I was getting. They said I was batting carelessly.

I was scoring runs in the matches against the counties and the MCC, including three centuries, and my total of 1644 runs for the tour was the highest in the party. Their advice was well meant and they had a point, but I told them: 'It's not that so much as me not getting the same luck as some of the other players. Other players are playing their shots like I am but are getting away with it. The first time I play the ball in the air near a fielder, he makes a great chance.'

I think I showed Clyde at the Oval in the Fifth Test that I had the necessary concentration to succeed on a bad pitch, scoring 39 out of the West Indies first-innings 89 and 42 out of the second-innings 88.

There were no coaches in Barbados when I first played cricket. We learned from watching the many good players playing in club and colonial matches. There was no television, either. We saw the players in person. Or we played with them in the roads, on pieces of spare land or on the beaches.

Beach cricket teaches the batsman how to take on quick bowlers, how to hook them. Two sticks are pitched in the wet sand where the tide comes in and the bowler bowls with a rubber or tennis ball which skids through, often at chest height. Nearly all the leading players in Barbados have played it.

I learned by studying how good players conducted themselves. I watched how they got close to the line of the ball and tried to follow their example. The first essential was to be keen, to want to learn. And the next one was to practise as much as possible. I was always at the nets working to improve myself.

Some of the senior players would put a coin on the stumps and challenge me to knock it off by hitting the stump. I learned the importance of accuracy, of change of pace and varying my flight.

I do not claim that when I became an established Test player I practised any harder than my team mates. But I worked very hard in my formative years. That is when the foundations were laid.

4 | The Boy from Bay Land

I was born on 28 July, 1936 at 3.30 in a small wooden house in Walcott Avenue, Bay Land, in the parish of St Michael, Barbados, the fifth child of Mr and Mrs Shamont Sobers. My father, a merchant seaman, decided I would be called Garfield St Auburn Sobers. Most Barbadians have unusual names, and I was no exception.

Thelma, my mother, told me that 'Garfield' was probably taken from a distant relative of my father's in the United States, but there was a suggestion that I was named after John Garfield, the American actor of the forties. I don't know about that, but I do know my sister Greta was named after Greta Garbo because my father admired her. The second name, 'St Auburn', was also supposed to come from an American relative. I do not bother about looking into how names were handed down.

I had two elder brothers, George and Gerry, younger brother Cecil and a sister called Elise. A seventh child died in infancy, the victim of an accident with a kerosene lamp. We did not see a lot of our father because he was away at sea most of the time, working for the Canadian 'Lady' ships transporting supplies to and from Barbados. We had no money for luxuries, only for necessities, but we were happy, well fed and adequately clothed. My father was a footballer and he occasionally played cricket. He was also a troop leader in the YMCA Scout troop. He would play cricket with us alongside the house, or at the back at Bay Pasture, an open common where the Wanderers Cricket Club had their ground before moving to their present ground in Dayrell's Road.

Sometimes he would bring soft balls back from England. Right from the age of three, sport dominated my life. When I was five, my father's ship, *The Lady Hawkins*, was torpedoed by a German submarine and was sunk with all hands. I do not remember too much about how the news was brought to us except that it was a sad time.

My mother had only a small pension from the Canadian government to bring up the family and she did such a magnificent job that we all turned out to be happy and successful in our chosen careers. None of us had a serious illness, and she devoted the whole of her life to us. No children could have had a more caring, loving and Christian mother. She always said she never contemplated marrying again because she feared that her new husband might mistreat the children.

George, my eldest brother, was given a Vestry Exhibition to Combermere School, the secondary school which had Sir Frank Worrell and Wes Hall on its roll. When he was fifteen he left school and worked as a meter-reader for the Barbados Electric Company. The extra income he brought in helped my mother provide for us in hard times.

Gerry, one year senior to me, and I went to Bay Street Boys' School (now moved to a new site) where we were fortunate to meet Everton Barrow, the sports master. Everton was a good club cricketer with the Empire Club and he gave us a lot of encouragement. 'You're going to have a big future in cricket,' he used to tell me.

Neither of us was a good scholar. We spent too much time playing cricket, tennis, water polo and other sports. Owing to a slight slanting of our eyes, we became known as 'the Chinese brothers'.

We spent hours every day until it was dark knocking balls around. Sometimes my mother would tell us to come in. She did not think it right that boys should play cricket in the road outside or in the gap between the houses. So we played cricket inside the house – with disastrous results for the furnishings.

Up to the age of eight or nine we used to play 'knee' cricket. The bat, which was about a couple of feet in length, was carved from the spine of a coconut branch or a paling taken from a wooden fence. The ball was a small stone with some layers of cloth wrapped around it and bound with a marlin cord. The finished product would be rolled in tar and left to dry.

It was surprising how long these home-made balls lasted on the bare rock-hard pitch at the back of the school. The owner of the ball was the important boy, so he usually went in first. With up to twenty or thirty fielders, no one batted long.

The batsman had to bat with his knee grounded just behind the crease. If you raised it after completing your stroke, you were liable to be stumped. Batting from this position encouraged square cutting and hooking – and many great West Indian cricketers, including Rohan Kanhai and Clive Lloyd, have shown their origins by playing shots on one knee in Test matches.

The bowler had to bowl underarm, which rather restricted him. I soon learned to spin the ball. There were no umpires. Decisions were usually made by those who could shout loudest. Our house was a short walk from the school, and we would try to get back early from lunch to continue our matches, which were always between sides named after English counties like Kent and Sussex. Our mother did her best to stop us. 'You take your time and give the food a chance to settle in your stomach,' she used to say.

Gerry was the best batsman in the school team which won the Inter-School Cricket Championship for primary schools three years in succession. I was looked upon as more of a bowler. Our toughest opponents were usually St Giles, the school attended by Wes Hall.

At weekends, we played for the Bay Land unofficial team at the pasture – or 'Brisbane', as we termed it. Our opponents were teams from other groups of boys who lived nearby, one led by Cammie Smith, later to become a Test opener. There were four sets of brothers in our team, and three of us became League cricketers in England: Gerry and myself and Keith Barker. We played all kinds of games – football, a home-made version of tennis and marbles.

Several afternoons I used to watch the cricketers at the Wanderers Club practising for the matches over the weekend. George Challenor, one of the great West Indian players, came from

Wanderers. During club matches, I did the scoring on the score-board, and so did Roy Marshall who later joined Hampshire. The groundsman at the time was Briggs Grandison, and we used to talk to him most days.

One of the members of the Wanderers team was the all-rounder Denis Atkinson, who toured India in 1948 with the West Indies. Before the tour started, Denis wanted to practise against a slow left-arm bowler to prepare himself for his coming meetings with Vinoo Mankad, the Indian spinner. Briggs told him that I would be able to bowl to him. I was twelve at the time. I gather at first Denis did not take the proposition seriously, but Briggs talked him into it.

Denis and some of the other members must have been reasonably impressed, for they asked me to bowl to them the following week. They would place a fifty-cent coin on the middle stump, and it was mine if I succeeded in bowling them. I earned enough money to be able to go to the Saturday-morning cinema-show in town. My heroes were the cowboys Tim Holt and Jimmy Wateley. Sometimes I earned enough to be able to treat some of my friends.

A few years later I would be playing with Denis in the West Indies side. I spent hours bowling in the Wanderers nets, the workshop where I first learned my trade.

By the time I was fourteen I had left school and was helping out in a furniture-making workshop run by Lionel Daniel overlooking the Wanderers ground. Lionel and his three brothers played football for Notre Dame, one of the leading clubs in Barbados, and intro-duced me to the club. I played at outside left and then in goal and was capped by Barbados in an inter-island match. Later, when it became clear that Everton Barrow's forecast that I would succeed in cricket was about to be realised, the Barbados Cricket Association advised me to stick to cricket and drop my football career.

I took their advice, because whereas football was amateur those who succeeded in cricket were professionals and made their living abroad. Cricket provided an exit and a way to make money. There was no finer way for a black boy to make a better life for himself.

Throughout my childhood I was fortunate to be helped by a number of people whom Trevor Bailey, author of a book about me in 1976, has called father figures. I suppose they were, and I shall always be indebted to them. One of the earliest to figure in my life was Goulbourne Cumberbatch, who lived in our road and became a friend and adviser. I spent many happy hours in his home, and it was 'Dada', as we called him, who taught me to play dominoes. Known to his friends as 'Goalie', he was a stevedore in Bridgetown harbour. It was 'Dada' who got me a brief job as a tally clerk at the harbour before I took up cricket professionally.

Another was Garnett Ashby, a builder who was a friend of Briggs Grandison. One day the Bay Land team run by Briggs was short, and another boy and I were invited to make up the numbers. The opponents were Kent, a country-district side captained by Garnett.

Bowling in short trousers, I took two early wickets, coming on as first change. Then I dismissed Garnett, and afterwards he asked me if I would like to play for Kent. The snag was that their ground, located in a village known as Penny Hole, was twelve miles from my house and, though I was agreeable, Garnett first had to seek permission from my mother. It was an awkward journey, and Garnett was proposing to take me on his motorcycle.

His first meeting with my mother was not very productive. 'You want to carry Garfield on the back of a motorcycle to the country to play cricket against big able men, and on a Sunday, too?' she said. 'I don't see how you could even think of asking me such a question. I don't even know you, my gentleman.'

Garnett had to recruit my brother George, my schoolteacher Everton Barrow, Briggs Grandison and a priest to support his arguments, and after five weeks my mother relented. Garnett proposed that I stay with him at the weekend. He had seven children and he treated me like one of them.

On the first journey to St Philip, where Penny Hole was situated, Garnett stopped at a shop to meet yet another man who was to be helpful to me: Johnny Webster, father of Dr Rudi Webster, the former Barbados and Warwickshire bowler. Garnett introduced me. 'This is the youngster I was telling you about,' he said.

Mr Webster, who owned part of the land on which the ground was situated and acted as a kind of patron, helping to pay the

subscriptions and expenses of the players, appeared a little surprised to see such a small boy.

'You're the person who always used to tell me that you mustn't
judge a book by its cover,' said Garnett. 'Don't take him by his
looks, boy. Before this match is finished you're going to think
differently.'

'All right,' said Mr Webster. 'It's only I was looking for someone
in long pants.'

Kent were a good side, the best team in the parish of St Philip for
three seasons and a respected member of the Barbados Cricket
League. The ground, reached by an unmade road in those days, was
about fifty yards from the road close to St Martin's Church, which
had a steeple before it was blown down by Hurricane Janet in 1955.

The opposition that day was a team called Trinity, and we played
a two-day match over the weekend against them. Garnett intro-
duced me to the players, and they all had a few welcoming words
which made me much less nervous.

Kent won the toss and batted and, going in at number ten, I made
9 not out. Trinity replied with 170, with my bowling figures 2–19.
There was a fair crowd, including a number of vendors, gathered in
the shade of the trees on one side of the ground. In Kent's second
innings we lost 6 wickets for 87, and Garnett promoted me to take
on Ralph Trotman, the Trinity bowler who was taking all the
wickets. I remember I hit his first deliveries for four and Mr Webster
came on to shake my hand while the field was changing over! I
finished with 29 and in Trinity's second innings, with Trinity's last
wicket going down with 9 runs still wanted, I took 4–35.

The late Michie Hewitt, founder of the Barbados Cricket League,
had quickly registered me to play for Kent, and I had a very happy
year and a half with them. Organised cricket started in Barbados
with the Barbados Cricket Association, which at first was mainly
confined to upper-class and leading schools.

Michie, a newspaper subeditor and columnist who was given the
OBE for his services to Barbados and West Indian cricket, did not
think this was fair, and in an attempt to widen the game to include
youngsters of all ages and classes was instrumental in forming the

Barbados Cricket League. Out of this new League were to come players like Everton Weekes, Conrad Hunte, Charlie Griffith, Seymour Nurse, Frank King, Clairmonte Depeiza and Vanburn Holder.

Once a year a match was played between the BCA and the BCL, and in my first year at Kent I was selected for the BCL team at the Empire Cricket Club, the ground where Frank Worrell had learned his cricket.

Before being selected for the BCL team there had been another vital stage of my career: my introduction to Captain Wilfrid Farmer, a police inspector who was captain of the Police cricket team and a former member of Wanderers. His son Stephen currently plays for Wanderers and has been a valuable member of the Barbados team.

The introduction was made by Denis Atkinson. I managed to bowl Captain Farmer out in the nets, and a week later he asked me: 'How would you like to play first-eleven cricket? I could get you into the Police band and that would qualify you to play for the team.' I had never played an instrument in my life but accepted the offer as first-team cricket was the next step up.

The following Monday I reported to St Cecilia Barracks to be drafted into the band as a bugler. I never did master that bugle!

My first match for Police was against Empire, one the strongest and most famous clubs in Barbados, at their ground at Bank Hall. They say they used to use candlegrease to prepare the pitch, and it was as fast as any I ever played on. Some of the great West Indian fast bowlers, including Herman Griffith, Manny Martindale and Charlie Griffith, learned their trade on that pitch.

I was number eight in the order and when I went to the wicket, in short trousers still because I was only five feet four inches, the bowler was E. A. V. Williams, who was known as 'Foffie'. He and Manny Martindale were rated the fastest pair of bowlers in the Caribbean and, though he was in his late thirties at the time, 'Foffie' was still very quick.

The first ball was straight, and I got behind it and played it back to the bowler. The second was wider, and I played it behind square on the off side for two. I tried a cut at the third ball, and it flew to the boundary. I do not think 'Foffie' was impressed. Next ball, a short delivery, I tried to hook and was struck in the mouth. I had to be assisted off the field. That was the moment when I came of age as a cricketer. I had been knocked down by one of the best bowlers in the West Indies, but it didn't frighten me. I was ready to start again – and the next bouncer would go out of the ground!

My stay in the band was a brief one, for after being hit in the mouth I was unable to play the instrument and failed to turn up for the next few days. The bandmaster was unimpressed by my explanation and announced that he had someone else to take my place.

Captain Farmer was undaunted. He arranged for me to join the Police Boys Club, which would still qualify me to play cricket for Police. By now I was sixteen and in long trousers. At school one of my best friends, Charlie Daniel, had a bet with me over which of us would be first to score a hundred in first-team cricket. My first century, 113 against Wanderers, came on the same day he scored his against Rangers.

Within a season I was picked for Barbados as a slow left-hand bowler, playing with Clyde Walcott and Everton Weekes, who gave me my first proper bat. Police were to remain my club side throughout my career. Whenever I was back in Barbados during the cricket season I would play for them. I started when I was fifteen and played my last game when I was forty-one.

Basketball became my second-favourite sport after I was asked to drop out of football. Gerry and I played for the Police team and enjoyed it. I loved playing sport and still do. I try to play as much golf as I can.

5 | Test Début

I was playing cricket with my brothers in the road outside my home in Walcott Avenue in March 1954 when Ben Hoyos, secretary of the Barbados Cricket Association, sent a message to my home saying I had been picked as a replacement for the final Test in Jamaica against England in a few days' time.

In those days the Sobers family had no telephone, which was why Ben had to send a message. Soon the whole neighbourhood knew, and everyone was terribly excited. I gathered together my gear, the pads which had been given to me by the Association and the Herbert Sutcliffe bat presented to me by Everton Weekes, and prepared to make my first flight in an aircraft. It was to be the first time I had left Barbados.

I had only played a handful of first-class matches, but the call-up did not surprise me too much. I was a confident young man! I was half-expecting to be asked to make my début after my success for Barbados against the Indians the year before when I bowled 89 overs and took 7 wickets for 142 runs.

The prize wicket among them was Polly Umrigar's. Polly was a powerful batsman who averaged 42 in 59 Tests, and when the late John Goddard, the Barbados captain, handed me the ball Polly pulled one of my early deliveries on to the roof of the Kensington stand at mid-wicket. No batsman had ever struck any of my deliveries that far before, but I was not downhearted. It made me more determined to get him out.

Umrigar and Vijay Hazare, another top-class batsman, scored reasonably freely, but with runs to play with (Barbados made 606–7 and *Wisden* recorded that 'H. Sobers' was not out 7)

Goddard kept me on. I didn't spin the ball much in those days, and most of my 7 wickets came from the straight ball or the arm ball, the one that drifted in from the off.

It was an arm ball, I remember, which dismissed Umrigar and gave me my first wicket in first-class cricket. It went between bat and pad and bowled him for 63.

I played in that match because Frank King, the only Test-class West Indies fast bowler of that era, was feeling tired and the selectors wanted to keep him fresh for the Second Test, which was due to start two days after the colony match ended.

And I was also a stand-in when I was called up for my début in Test cricket a year later. Alf Valentine was injured, and I was the next slow left-hand bowler in line.

I was 17 years and 245 days old, the tenth-youngest cricketer to make his début in Test cricket. The youngest, Pakistani Mushtaq Mohammad (15 and 124 days) went on to play Test cricket for seventeen years, but I managed twenty! The three youngest Test players, Aftab Baloch, Nasim-ul-Ghani and Khalid Hassan were all Pakistanis. The statistics show that Pakistan, India and the West Indies have traditionally given an early start to their players. England, the home of cricket, is more conservative. Brian Close was the youngest debutant at 18 years 149 days.

I remember I was not over-awed despite playing alongside my heroes, Clyde Walcott, Everton Weekes and Frank Worrell. I had met Everton a year earlier at the trial game before the Barbados squad was picked. Everton asked one of the other players: 'Who is that little fellow?'

'That's Garry Sobers, our youngest player,' the player replied.

Everton grinned. 'Sobers, eh?' he said, turning to me. 'Hello, Soapbox!'

The England side was skippered by Len Hutton and included such names as Peter May, Denis Compton, Tom Graveney, Godfrey Evans, Jim Laker, Tony Lock and Fred Trueman, who was being called 'fiery' by the critics.

Fred, whom I soon came to admire as one of the greatest competitors I played against, was very quick and occasionally erratic. It was his first tour, and I believe he upset a few people off the field with his Yorkshire bluntness! It had not been a happy tour for the team generally. They were angry about some of the umpiring decisions. The scoring was frequently slow by the Englishmen, and in one Test both sides resorted to bowling at the leg stump.

By the time the final Test came round the West Indies led 2–1 and needed a draw to clinch the rubber. Jeffrey Stollmeyer, our captain, won the toss and decided to bat. 'You're number nine,' he told me. I expected to have a quiet first day watching our batsmen in action. But Trevor Bailey proceeded to take three quick wickets, and the score was 110–7 when I went in. I do not remember feeling too tense. After all, I had been picked as a bowler not as a batsman, so there was less pressure on me. The brochure being sold around the ground described me as 'a useful batsman'. I wanted to prove that I was better than that!

The two bowlers in action were Bailey and Fred Trueman and it was very difficult to understand why we had lost so many wickets. The pitch was good and the light perfect. Trevor was not a bowler who did a lot with the ball. He was quickish and moved it about off the seam, a little bit this way and a little bit the other way. He finished with 7–34, and we were all out 139. I was 14 not out, the only occasion in my Test career when I ran out of partners. I was constantly criticised during my captaincy for putting myself too low in the order, but I was never left stranded.

When I arrived back in the dressing-room in Kingston the other players responded as though I had made a century. Most of them congratulated me. It gave me added confidence when it came to bowling the next day. Len Hutton opened with Trevor Bailey, later to become a personal friend, and Trevor thus achieved the unique experience of opening both batting and bowling in a Test on the same day.

Frank King and Gerry Gomez used the new ball, and after Denis Atkinson and Sonny Ramadhin failed to make the breakthrough Stollmeyer threw it to me. With the fourth ball of my first over, Trevor attempted a square cut, thinking the ball was leaving him, and was caught behind by Clifford McWatt for his first Test wicket. 'I played for the turn which wasn't there,' he said.

That was my last success for some time, because Hutton batted like a master and his 205 out of England's 414 enabled his team to win by 9 wickets to square the series. I had the satisfaction of having the best bowling figures: 4–74 off 28.5 overs. My other victims were the England spin trio of Johnny Wardle, Jim Laker and Tony Lock.

Wardle was a fine attacking bowler whose career was over-shadowed by Lock's. If Lock hadn't been around, Wardle would have played many more than 28 Tests.

Trevor Bailey was one of England's best-ever all-rounders at a time when England did not have many of them. Ian Botham has been the number one Englishman in this department in terms of figures, and I would rate Trevor in the next group behind him along with Tony Greig, Basil d'Oliveira and Ray Illingworth.

As a batsman, he was cautious and reliable. His forward defens-ive shot was his trademark, and he never conceded his wicket without a fight. If he made a big score, you could be sure it would take a long time. He was a sound catcher in the field. He usually fielded close to the wicket. I cannot envisage him racing around the boundary to make a diving save!

Batsmen of Trevor's stubborn approach were commonplace in English cricket when I played in England, both as a Test player and with Nottinghamshire in the county championship. Whereas the West Indian batsman wants to hit the ball – 'give it some licks' we say – the English batsman is more concerned about survival.

Ken Barrington's experience in his early days is well known – how he started out his Test career as a shotmaker only to be dropped as too unreliable. Kenny set out to let his figures provide the evidence that he was worth a recall, and several years later restarted his Test career as a dour defensive player. He was still capable of playing exciting shots, but most of the time they were locked away.

I do not believe it was the fault of the players that they become dull players. They were victims of the system of selection. The

selectors looked at the averages and usually picked the men who
were near the top.

Brian Bolus, the Yorkshireman who played with me at Nottinghamshire and eventually succeeded me as captain, was a similar
player. When he made his England début against the West Indies in
1963 he scored 105 runs for an average of 26, twice scoring 43 in
quick time. That winter he was England's leading run-getter in the
series in India with 391 runs, average 48, yet was never picked
again.

His whole approach changed, and he was so cautious that he was
christened 'Paddy' Bolus because he was always using his pads. I
believe Phil Sharpe, now an England selector, was another attractive batsman who was caught up in this predicament of having to
eliminate most of his shots to enhance his Test career.

English cricketers have long had to worry about producing the
figures to satisfy committees at the end of their contracts. Cricket as
a profession is an insecure one in any part of the world, but it seems
to be more so in England.

Most great players will not worry. They will make the runs
whatever the pressure. But for ordinary players it is a strain, and it is
reflected in the way they play the game.

My next experience of Test cricket came in 1955 when the
Australians under Ian Johnson visited the Caribbean. They were
unbeaten, having won three of the Tests with two drawn, and
proved to be popular wherever they went. The Australian is closer
to the West Indian in his approach to the game. He cannot just
survive at the crease, or slow the over rate down to suit a tactical
plan. He wants to hit the ball and get on with the action. It was an
exciting time for me, because it was my first glimpse of the great
fast-bowling pair Keith Miller and Ray Lindwall. These two
wonderful sportsmen each took 20 wickets and caused havoc with
their bouncers. In those days umpires rarely warned bowlers about
bowling too many. There were no experimental rules about one per
over.

With outstanding hookers like Everton Weekes, the best hooker I
have seen, and Clyde Walcott in the West Indies side, there was

some exciting cricket. We were beaten chiefly because our bowling wasn't as good as theirs. Our fastest bowler, Frank King, only managed to take 3 wickets at 134 apiece.

During one of the Tests, Miller and Lindwall, who had been out that night, knocked on my door at midnight. I was sharing with Collie Smith, and we were apprehensive about what was happening.

'We know you are in there,' Keith said. 'Open up or we'll knock the door down.' He wanted to come in and share a drink with us!

I think it was that occasion when Keith gave Collie some useful advice. 'If you get hundreds, don't think you've made it,' he said. 'In this game you could get a pair in your next Test. Don't believe what the newspapers say when they hail your successes. Bear in mind it could just as easily come unstuck.'

That was something I was never to forget. I learned a lot from them that night. And Keith's words were to prove prophetic because in the next Test Collie made a pair – scored 0 in both innings – and was promptly dropped!

I was nineteen and impressionable, and that made a greater impression on me than anything. When the tour was over Keith Miller gave me his bat, a 'White Toe' model. It had a white strip across the bottom. He was a most generous person, and still is.

The West Indies were not a team in those days as they are today. Frank Worrell had still to weld the different units together and build the team spirit which I and Clive Lloyd strove – successfully, I think – to maintain.

There was friction between the islands about selections, and nineteen players were used in the series, including three different wicket-keepers in the first three Tests. Collie Smith, one of the certainties to develop into a great player, was dropped and so were Sonny Ramadhin and Alf Valentine.

There was also a bitter controversy about the captaincy when Jeff Stollmeyer missed the First, Fourth and Fifth Tests. The choice was Denis Atkinson, a Barbadian insurance salesman who I had known from my days at Wanderers. A campaign developed in Jamaica and several other islands to have him deposed and Frank Worrell appointed instead.

Denis showed he was well worth his place by scoring 219 and taking 5 wickets in the second innings in the Bridgetown Test. He was a good medium-pace bowler who bowled off-cutters, and a hard-hitting batsman.

His stand with wicket-keeper Clairmonte Depeiza (122) set a Test record of 348 for the seventh wicket. Depeiza, a Customs clerk, had never scored a first-class hundred and, as the milestone approached, the Barbadian crowd became more and more excited. Miller and Lindwall bowled a succession of bouncers, and Depeiza – nicknamed 'The Leaning Tower of Depeiza' by the spectators because of the way he kept leaning forward into his defensive prod – was struck a number of painful blows on the chest. During a break in play John Goddard senior, father of the Test captain of the same name, produced a piece of foam rubber which he suggested Depeiza should wear as protection. It was the first time I had heard of chest protectors. Now they are commonplace. The fans collected $1000 for Depeiza.

Australia piled up 668 in their first innings, and there was a lot of argument in the crowd about who would open the innings for the West Indies. J. K. Holt, the regular opener, had been barracked for dropping a number of catches and was lacking in confidence. One of his Jamaican countrymen, former West Indies fast bowler Leslie Hylton, was in gaol waiting to be hanged for the murder of his wife at the time, and banners went up at Kensington Oval saying: 'Save Hylton, hang Holt.'

Clairmonte had been another contender, but he had failed in the preceding tourists' match against Barbados. I was amazed when Denis Atkinson came to me as he came off the field and said: 'You had better get your pads on, lad; you're going to open.' I had never opened the innings at any level, and I felt that I was being sacrificed to protect the 'three Ws'.

Not that I argued. I relished the prospect of facing Miller and Lindwall. Holt took strike from Lindwall's first over, which left me to face Miller, the faster, more dynamic and unpredictable of the two. Lindwall's arm was lower. Miller's was high, and he bounced the ball more. I decided I would not be too reticent. I hooked a four to fine leg, another through the covers and a third past point in the first over. The crowd loved it, whistling and shouting with delight.

In Keith's next over, I hit him for three more fours, all through the covers. Ray Lindwall smiled at me. 'Good going, son,' he said. 'But mind you stay this end!' When he took the first wicket, yorking Holt, the total was 52 and we hadn't changed ends.

Keith came off, replaced by Johnson, the skipper. I swept Ian for my tenth four (out of 43) and, trying another sweep, top-edged to Jack Hill about forty-five yards away at backward square leg. Whenever I see Ian now in Melbourne, where he has retired as secretary of the Melbourne Cricket Club, he says: 'Hey, there's my rabbit. You know you kept me in cricket longer than I should have been.'

There was an incident in that match that reveals the spirit those Tests were played in. During the Atkinson–Depeiza stand, Atkinson, thinking the ball was dead, walked down the pitch to chat to his partner. Keith picked it up, walked to the stumps and said: 'You know I could have run you out, Denis.' He laughed, and so did Denis.

Miller and Lindwall were not as quick as they had been in England in 1948, but on the firmer, bouncier West Indies pitches they were the most hostile bowlers I had seen up to then. None of today's fast bowlers was any faster or more dangerous. The difference was that there were only two of them compared with the four in the West Indies side which became world champions under Clive Lloyd.

Ron Archer, fast medium, was the back-up, followed by the guile of Richie Benaud and the flighted off-breaks of Ian Johnson. The West Indies fast-bowling response was in the hands of one man, Frank King.

King had as elegant an action as Michael Holding, and his pace was not far short of Wes Hall's. Wes, who started out as a wicket-keeper batsman, was so impressed with his run-up that he copied it. Wes was in the first team at Combermere School when Frank was the groundsman so the similarities were not coincidental. Frank was tall and slim like Holding and used to glide up to the crease on his toes, almost like a ballet dancer. Everything about his action was right.

He was so over-bowled that he constantly had injury problems. If he had had someone to back him up at the other end, he would have been one of the leading wicket-takers in West Indies cricket.

Lindwall (118) and Miller (137) both scored centuries in that Bridgetown Test; and Miller, as good an all-rounder as I have ever played with, finished with a batting average of 73. Walcott made five centuries in his 827 runs and was the most successful of the 'Ws' at that time. Each of them had his own distinctive style: Clyde was powerful and commanding; Everton Weekes, smaller in build, equally powerful of shot; and Frank Worrell graceful and stylish.

My favourite as a batsman was Everton Weekes. I loved to see him bat. Clyde was also a great player. There was no doubting that. And Frank was the best leader of men I ever played with.

My own contribution was unexceptional – 231 runs, average 38, and 6 wickets at 35 apiece. But I learned a lot from Miller and Lindwall. My education was continuing.

Keith Miller had warned me about the pitfalls to come, and they arrived sooner than I expected – in New Zealand in 1955–6. It was the first of three visits I made to New Zealand, and each time I had a miserable time on the field.

The pitches were under-prepared in 1955–6, and coming from the flat easy batting-surfaces of the Caribbean I found I was unable to adjust. My top score was a mere 27 and I averaged just 16. For some reason Denis Atkinson put me in at number three and kept me there. My form did not justify such a high position.

The West Indies won the series easily enough with a largely experimental side, but the New Zealanders had some fine players. Their captain, John Reid, was an excellent medium-pacer and an aggressive hitter of the ball. He went to England to play League cricket, yet failed to get the same worldwide exposure as his successor as all-rounder in the modern era, Richard Hadlee.

Hadlee was a better bowler, but there was not much to choose between them as all-round cricketers. And I also rated another all-rounder, Bruce Taylor, a tall, brisk bowler who tried to get batsmen out with every delivery no matter how tough he found the conditions. Bruce troubled me a lot in the 1968–9 series and also bowled extremely well in the West Indies.

Bev Congdon, Hedley Howarth, Dick Motz, Richard Collinge and Geoff Howarth, a fine skipper, were all worthy Test players, and New Zealand had to be taken seriously by the other nations.

Some of our players in 1955–6 liked New Zealand so much that they settled there. Opener Bruce Pairaudeau did, and so did wicket-keeper Simpson Guillen, who became one of the few players to represent two countries at Test level, playing for New Zealand against the West Indies in 1956.

6 | The Day They Stopped Ram

My first tour of England was in 1957, and it was my first experience of English 'professionalism'. The mystery West Indian spin bowler Sonny Ramadhin had bowled England to defeat in the 1950 series, in company with the Jamaican slow left-hander Alf Valentine who spun the ball so viciously that it hummed through the air.

Seven years on, Ram was twenty-eight and ready to take more wickets. He was still a great bowler, and the best of the world's batsmen had still to solve his mysteries. England's players must have spent a long time deciding how to combat him, and we saw their answer in the second innings of the First Test at Edgbaston.

Ram's wrist used to flick over so quickly that it was almost impossible to see which way the ball was turning as it left his hand. Was he a leg-spinner who could bowl googlies? Or was he a bowler who bowled both off-breaks and leg-breaks with the same action?

A neat tidy person, he always had his shirt-sleeves buttoned down, which added to the deception. Some spin bowlers, particularly in India, bowl with the sleeve flapping, but that was not Ram's style. If the sleeve is loose, the batsman has the right to ask the bowler to button it up if he feels it distracts him. Ram was a likeable person. He wouldn't have wanted to try to take advantage of anyone.

Ram was a golf caddy in Duncan Village in the south of Trinidad when he first started playing cricket. I never really discussed it with him, but I have a feeling he first learned the art of spin with a golf ball. Word soon spread that there was a youngster playing in the south who was bowling a lot of good batsmen out and they couldn't read him. Two selectors, Jeff Stollmeyer and Derek Sealy, took a look at him, liked what they saw, and he was chosen for two trial games. On the strength of that he was picked for the 1950 tour of England. It was the quickest rise to fame of any young cricketer.

Ram never bowled a googly, and it took England's batsmen a long time to work that out. He bowled either the off-break or the leg-break. His palm was pointing down the pitch at the batsman as he bowled, and his arm and wrist came over so quickly that the batsman was unable to pick which way the ball was going in the air.

If you played a few shots against him and gave the impression you had read him, he could lose confidence. But I never met many batsmen, or wicket-keepers, who could confidently predict which way the ball would be turning. On true pitches, he didn't turn the ball a lot. Just enough.

When we arrived in Birmingham the feeling in the team was that we might well repeat the success of 1950. The 'three Ws' were still there, so were Ram and Val, and they were joined by younger players like Rohan Kanhai, Collie Smith, Roy Gilchrist, Wes Hall and myself.

Ram was at his baffling best in the England first innings, taking 7–49 in 31 overs. England were all out 186, and our first-innings 474 put us in a commanding position. I reached 50 in my first Test innings in England, only to be brilliantly caught diving to his left by my friend Trevor Bailey. Collie Smith batted brilliantly for his 161.

Clyde Walcott pulled a muscle and needed a runner; Frank Worrell also needed a runner; and Roy Gilchrist, our only fast bowler, ricked his ankle but was forced to continue. On the fourth day, Peter May and Colin Cowdrey came together twenty minutes after the start of play, and more than eight hours were to pass before we took another wicket.

Ram bowled unchanged a marathon 98 overs, and for most of the time May and Cowdrey stuck their left leg down the pitch, bat and pad close together, and padded his deliveries away. If the ball turned in to them, they reasoned that the umpires, Emrys Davies and Charlie Elliott, wouldn't be able to give them out. If it was a leg-break, they wouldn't be out anyway. Surely some of our many appeals HAD to be out!

It was one of the most depressing sights I have seen in Test cricket. The game is meant to be played with the bat, not with the pad. The crowd didn't mind. The fourth-wicket stand of 411, a record in Tests, had saved England, and the total of 583–4 even enabled May to come close to victory. We were holding on at 72–7 at the end. Ram was never the same bowler. He took only five more wickets in the series. He had been destroyed by a theory, a theory which worked. But it wasn't cricket.

Yet it might have all been different if skipper John Goddard had taken the new ball in England's second innings. We were so short of bowlers that Goddard decided that Ram would have to keep going, so he declined the opportunity of taking another new ball.

One of the senior players said to him: 'Let Garry try his quicker bowling.' Up to then I hadn't bowled quickly in a match. That was to come in Australia in 1960–1. But I bowled fast in the nets, and the players knew what I could do. Goddard rejected the idea, and Ram carried on with a ball which was getting softer all the time. We used that ball for 162 overs. Ridiculous! A new ball would have bounced more and changed the tempo of the game. It might have given May and Cowdrey a few more problems.

England had a powerful team in those days, one of their best line-ups of postwar years. Their attack was balanced, unlike ours, with Brian Statham partnering Fred Trueman with the new ball, Trevor Bailey first change and the spin bowling in the hands of Jim Laker and Tony Lock, the finest pair of spinners any country had in those days.

Bailey's 7–44 at Lord's in the Second Test, watched in the five days by 98,985 people – more than can be accommodated at the ground today – saw the West Indies lose again, this time by an innings and 36 runs, and the series was virtually over. We dropped twelve chances in England's first-innings 424, and Godfrey Evans must have been missed at least eight times in his 82. I was guilty myself. No one escaped. Poor Gilchrist was inconsolable.

The difference between that West Indies side and today's – besides the greater number of fast bowlers now, four to the one we had in Gilchrist – was in fielding. Today the team takes most of its catches. In that particular series, we missed many more than we caught.

England had better catchers in the 1957 series. Cowdrey was a fine slipper, and Bailey had shown he could take difficult chances. We envied May being able to call on two fast bowlers while we were forced to use Frank Worrell as an opening bowler. Frank was a good bowler but he wasn't a quick bowler.

At the time it was said that Fred Trueman got many of his wickets because batsmen took chances against him after being pinned down at the other end by Brian Statham. 'George,' as Statham was nicknamed, was amazingly accurate. But I felt that his accuracy counted against him. The batsman could be sure where the ball would land. He was never likely to take anyone by surprise.

Trueman was more unpredictable, and in those days he bowled few bad balls. Later on he became one of the greatest fast bowlers in the game's history, rarely bowling a loose delivery. There was an element of truth in the 'Statham makes it easy for Fred' theory, because batsmen tried to chase Fred's deliveries sometimes if no boundaries were coming, and maybe he did pick up one or two extra wickets.

A feeling among some batsmen at the time was that if they could keep Statham out they could go for their shots against Trueman. The same philosophy was employed against the West Indies when first Frank King then Roy Gilchrist was our main strike bowler. I never believed in that. My approach was to try the opposite: attack the main bowler. If you forced him to be taken off, it would weaken the morale of the fielding side.

As Test sides recruited more and more fast bowlers, it became less easy to keep the best bowler or bowlers at bay. That was one of the secrets of the success of the West Indies side under Clive Lloyd once Andy Roberts and Michael Holding came off, Joel Garner, Colin Croft or Winston Davis was waiting to come on. There was no respite.

After our escape at Edgbaston, never a good venue for the West Indies, our team disintegrated and lost the series 3–0. Team spirit was bad. There were too many factions, and a number of key players lost form. Outside of the Tests, I was the team's most consistent scorer, but I wished I'd had more luck in the Tests.

May and Cowdrey both had successful series, but the man who topped the England batting averages was Tom Graveney, the best front-foot player I have ever played against. It was unbelievable that he was left out of the team for a number of years by the selectors. There was no cricketing explanation for this. Few English players approached his class. It must have been something he said.

In the final Test at the Oval, played on a pitch which Everton Weekes described as 'a beach', Tom made 164 out of England's 412. The combined totals mustered in both West Indies innings was 175! Perhaps if Valentine and Denis Atkinson had been fit it might have been more difficult for England's batsmen. They were both bowlers who pushed the ball through, and the pitch demanded that style of bowling.

Ram, Collie and myself bowled 127 overs between us, and critics of the present West Indies over rate would be amazed to learn that there were times in that series when we exceeded 20 overs an hour.

Val bowled the quickest over in my twenty years of Test cricket. Unless the ball was hit to the boundary, one of his overs would occupy between a minute and a minute and a half. I prided myself on being nearly as quick myself when bowling in my slower style. Later on, Lance Gibbs was to bowl his overs in two minutes or under.

We knew what to expect at the Oval when my second delivery to David Sheppard turned a foot, took the edge of the bat and flew between Gerry Alexander behind the wicket and Clyde Walcott at slip. I was not a great spinner of the ball, and that delivery must have made our batsmen apprehensive. If I could turn it that much, what would Laker and Lock do?

The previous year Laker had taken 19 wickets against the Australians on a similar pitch. I rated Jim the best off-spin bowler of my time, possibly of all time. England had a crop of good off-spinners at that time, including Ray Illingworth, Fred Titmus and the Gloucestershire pair David Allen and John Mortimore.

Laker was the number one undisputed champion. He had

immaculate control of line and length and knew the weaknesses of his opponents. His best ball was the one that left the batsman, the one that drifted away. It was bowled with the off-break action. My time batting against him in that Oval Test was an education for me. I top-scored in the first innings with 39 out of 89, and also in the second with 42 out of 86.

Earlier in the tour it was said by some players that I was too careless. Those two innings, in the most atrocious batting conditions against the world's most dangerous spin combination, showed that I could bat with discipline and restraint. Tony Lock bowled me in both innings. He was bowling in his fast, more questionable style in those days!

Lock took 11 wickets in the rout at the Oval. Time and time again he would make the ball turn and jump, hitting me on the chest or arm.

Lance Gibbs was the outstanding hard-wicket off-spin bowler of my time. He was a tall man, and with his high action obtained more bounce than most of his rivals. I would imagine that one in ten of his 309 Test victims, maybe more, were caught by me close in at leg slip.

The difference between Jim and Lance was that Jim would wheel away whatever the state of the game, tempting batsmen with his variations of flight and direction; while Lance, particularly later on in his career, would push the ball in quicker if he was being hit.

David Allen was a quality bowler, and I always thought John Mortimore was underrated. Titmus was similar to Illingworth - accurate and not easy to get away.

While England have always been able to produce good off-spinners, up to today's top exponent John Emburey, the Australians have had few, if any. Ashley Mallett was possibly the best I played against in Australia.

After the match was lost a tall distinguished-looking man came into our dressing-room. 'Well played, son,' he said. 'I've watched you all this series and know you are a better batsman than a bowler. You proved it today, for it needed something special to bat the way you did on that pitch. You will go from strength to strength, I am sure of it.'

Later someone told me he was Frank Woolley, reckoned to be England's greatest left-handed batsman of prewar years. He was also a left-arm spin bowler and a close catcher.

7 | Breaking the Record

I was twenty-one when I became the holder of the record for the highest individual score by a batsman in a Test match: 365 not out for the West Indies against Pakistan at Sabina Park on 3 March 1958.

Thirty years have passed, and no other batsman has got within 50 runs of that record. The closest was the former Australian captain Bobby Simpson with his 311 against England at Old Trafford in 1964.

Records are made to be broken, but I do not think mine will be beaten. I say that because the game has changed. With so many incentives on offer in the modern game, captains are less willing to bat a long time. One-day cricket is producing a type of batsman who is less capable of playing a very long innings. When the Pakistan batsman Javed Miandad scored 270 at the Oval in 1987 against England it was an exception. But there was no real risk that my record would be overtaken. There are few batsmen around with the necessary depth of concentration to stay at the crease for ten hours or more and aim for a score of 300 plus. Geoff Boycott might have had the concentration needed. However, he was too slow a scorer. The New Zealand batsman Martin Crowe has earned a reputation as being one of the outstanding of the younger batsmen and might eventually threaten my record, but I have not seen enough of him to judge.

Someone I thought might have had a chance was the South African Barry Richards whom I played against when I was captain of Nottinghamshire in the English county championship and he was with Hampshire. He was a great player. 'Great' is a misused word.

see it applied to so many players who have not qualified for such an accolade. David Gower played some fine innings early in his career and was immediately labelled 'great'. Greatness is achieved over a period of time – I would say ten years – and if a player has come up with consistent performances against the world's best bowlers in that time he can justifiably be called great.

I do not think David Gower, useful player as he is, has yet reached that standard. Greatness in batting is not about accumulating large totals at a cautious rate. It is about dominating bowling, and not just on good wickets. A great player will get the bowler to do what he wants him to do by his genius. He will improvise and play unorthodox shots to defeat the field.

Don Bradman did that, and he was the greatest of them all. But I do not think there have been too many great batsmen emerging since I began my career.

Graeme Pollock averaged 60 in the few Tests he was allowed to take part in, and I put him in the same class as Barry Richards: a potentially great player who was unable to confirm his stature because he did not play enough Test matches. Who knows? Perhaps either of them might have beaten my record had South Africa not been excluded from the family of cricketing nations.

One player who set many Test batting records was Sunil Gavaskar, the Indian batsman who I say was unquestionably a great player. He was still making hundreds in Test cricket when he announced his retirement at the age of 38 in 1987. His highest was 236 not out. Like all great players, Sunny took on the world's leading bowlers and got the better of them. He faced the stiffest tests and passed with honours. Thirteen of his record number of Test centuries came against the West Indies. I was the captain when he made his Test début against the West Indies in 1970 when he scored 774 runs, including four centuries.

Sunny had sound concentration and good technique, and when he was on top he controlled the game. He made good balls look bad and was never afraid to hook. Many of the best batsmen were of his diminutive size – Hanif, Rohan Kanhai, Lindsay Hassett, Neil Harvey, Everton Weekes and the best in history: Don Bradman.

Sunny passed 200 numerous times but never 300. Only ten men have done that: three Australians (Bradman did it twice with 334 and 304), four Englishmen, one Pakistani and two West Indians.

My West Indies colleague Lawrence Rowe became a contender in 1974 when he reached 302 against England in Bridgetown before Tony Greig had him caught. He was a fine player who might have done more than he did in the game. I remember the match well. It was not one of my happier matches.

Rohan Kanhai had me at seven in the order, and there was not much time left before the declaration when it was my turn to bat. It was not a time to send in a batsman, because if he survived he would have scored only a few runs – or nought. I scored a duck!

What was it like, playing in a Test match thirty years ago? The weather was brilliantly sunny, I remember that. The pitch was fast, faster than any Test pitch I had encountered. It was a batsman's game in those days. In the five Tests against Abdul Hafeez Kardar's Pakistan team the total number of runs scored was 6374.

In the First Test at Bridgetown, Hanif Mohammad, the little Pakistan opener, made 337, the second-highest individual total behind Sir Len Hutton's 364. He batted 16 hours 13 minutes, the longest Test innings. Hanif was a very correct player whose concentration was legendary. He didn't take many chances. He respected good balls and waited for the bad ones.

Hanif was and still is the holder of the highest first-class individual score in cricket of 499 in a Pakistan domestic match, in Karachi, beating Sir Don Bradman's 452. That is one record that I can't see being beaten! Not outside the subcontinent!

It was perhaps, one of cricket's ironies that Hanif should bowl the ball which I hit for the run which took me to 365. Hanif, more than any of his contemporaries, was favoured to be the batsman to dethrone Len Hutton. I do not imagine many people thought I would do it.

Before that Test match in Kingston I played 28 Test innings without passing the hundred mark. I had played in 17 Tests. Centuries had come in inter-island cricket and on tour but not in the arena where a batsman's true abilities are judged. Yet I was not too worried. I knew the barrier would soon be broken.

Many experts had forgotten that I began my Test career as a bowler, batting at number nine in the order. Earlier in 1957 I moved up to opener on occasions to partner my skipper Frank Worrell as a stand-in because the selectors were unhappy with Bruce Pairaudeau and Andy Ganteaume.

Against the Pakistanis, I was at number three, not my best position, but on such a good wicket and with so many good players in the side you wanted to get in as early as possible! I felt I was batting better in that series than at any time in my career. I had scored 183 not out for Barbados against the Pakistanis, who were touring the Caribbean for the first time.

Kardar won the toss at Sabina Park and decided to bat, as any skipper would. Pakistan scored 328, with opener Imtiaz Ahmed reaching 122. I had tremendous respect for Imtiaz, who was also the team's wicket-keeper. He struck the ball with great force, rarely moving his feet.

Conrad Hunte and Rohan Kanhai opened for the West Indies. Rohan wasn't really an opener, but the West Indies had still to find a partner for Conrad. He could be too impetuous, too easily riled by remarks from opposing players.

Not that the Pakistanis of that era set out to upset him. They spoke a different language, and their sportsmanship was unquestioned. They had no bowlers of great pace, but I am annoyed when some people claimed that their attack was lacking in depth and bowlers of any quality.

No one would dispute that Fazal Mahmood was a bowler of class. Three years earlier his bowling at the Oval enabled Pakistan to win their first match in England. Kardar, a slow left-arm bowler, was captain in that match. Fazal's opening partner was Mahmood Hussain, a useful medium-fast bowler. He broke down after delivering only five balls in his opening over and never bowled again in the match. First change was Khan Mohammad, quicker than either Fazal or Mahmood Hussain. Kardar's second-string spinner was Nasim-Ul-Ghani, who was the youngest-ever Test player when he made his début at the age of 16 years 248 days against us in Bridgetown. A year later he was to lose his record to Mushtaq Mohammad, who was 15 years 124 days when he made his début against us in Lahore.

Both Kardar and Nasim were injured, and poor Fazal had to bowl no fewer than 85 overs for figures of 2–247. Khan was more expensive: 259 off 54 overs!

The total was 87, the bad-luck number in Australia, when Kanhai was out and I walked to the wicket. Some matches you know that you will do well, and this was one of them. Conrad, one of the best opening batsmen the West Indies have ever had, if not the best, was batting beautifully. He had scored a century (142) on his début in the First Test in Bridgetown and was full of confidence.

Now he was to score another century. I soon followed him. I was concentrating so much that I remember little about it afterwards – the shot, the bowler or the reaction of the packed 20,000 crowd. I felt a sense of great relief; a vast obstacle in my career had been removed.

When play ended on the third day, I was 228 not out and Conrad was 242. As it was a six-day Test, there was time for one of us, or maybe both, to set a new individual Test record. Normally I sleep well when I eventually go to bed, admittedly later than most people, but on this occasion I had a restless night. Perhaps because of the talk of records and the possibilities the next day, I found myself lying awake. This was before the days when the team doctor gave players sleeping tablets!

I was not concerned about records. I never was at any time in my career. I felt I could bat on and on, and that no one could get me out. If that happened, I would be sure to beat the record – providing my captain, Gerry Alexander, did not declare.

Before we went out Conrad told me that we were within reach of the world record of 451 for the second wicket held by the Australians Don Bradman and Bill Ponsford. He mentioned the figure and, when we were one short of it, pushed a ball from Khan on the on side and called for a run. He was well out of his ground when the throw from substitute Aijaz Butt hit the stumps. Hunte made 260, his Test highest, and it was a tragedy because he could have got many, many more runs.

Later we discovered that the 'run' had been in vain. We had been 5 runs short of the record. Our stand was worth 446. Everton Weekes was next man in. What a man to come in at 533–2! He had been sitting with his pads on for many hours but he showed no sign of stiffness as he started to play his shots from the outset.

He hadn't been in long when he whipped a delivery from Khan out to mid-wicket and I set off on a run. I was horrified to see that Everton had not left his crease. Fortunately the fielder, Waqar Hussain, one of the two substitutes, threw to the wrong end! That was the only time I could have been out in my innings. It was a chanceless innings.

I celebrated my escape by passing 250 in 421 minutes, and soon the total of 576 had bettered the previous highest by the West Indies on the ground. The gates were shut, and the crowd was talking excitedly of the next record once I passed George Headley's 270, the previous highest by a West Indian. On the radio, Roy Lawrence was reminding hundreds of thousands of listeners that Hutton's record was in danger.

Everton went at 602–3, caught by Hanif at slip for 39 off Fazal. When Clyde Walcott came in, he told me that Gerry Alexander was thinking of declaring. As the West Indies were almost 300 ahead that made sense. 'Don't worry about it,' said Clyde. 'Settle down. Take it easy. The runs will come, and I will give you as much of the strike as I can.'

Clyde started with a two and a six off Fazal and then struck Karder, bowling with a broken finger, for one of the biggest sixes ever seen at Sabina Park. The ball soared over the stands and fell in Melbourne Road. Play had to be suspended for five minutes while it was retrieved.

The taking of the new ball accelerated the scoring, as usually happens when two batsmen are set. A single off Fazal took me to 300. I was the first West Indian to reach that figure in Tests. I had tried not to think of the figure 365, but it was now impossible not to do so. The way I approached it was that I didn't really have 300 on the board but was new to the crease and needed 64 to win the match.

I did not feel tired. My restless night had not affected me. The excitement had stimulated me. The runs kept coming. I felt good. The noise from the spectators, many in trees and on pylons, was incredible. They cheered the 100 stand, posted in 90 minutes. At tea the total was 730 for 3, with me on 336 and Walcott 58.

Two runs later I passed Hanif's 337, and he ran up from cover to shake my hand. I was told later that most people in Barbados were listening on their radios.

When I was on 363, Kardar asked Hanif to bowl for the first time. Hanif was not a bowler of note! Walcott took a single off his second delivery, and I faced him with the spectators shouting and baying. I needed to refrain from taking chances. I stroked the ball out to long off, and we ran a single. I was level with Hutton.

When I faced Hanif again, he asked the umpire if he could bowl left-handed. 'You can bowl with both hands if you like,' I said. I pushed his first ball into the covers, Clyde called, and off I went. Sabina Park was in a state of bedlam. There were no high fences then, and hundreds of spectators ran on to engulf me. I was overjoyed. It was something unique, something that may never happen again.

Suddenly I felt guilty that my success had reacted against my team. The skipper wouldn't like the hold-up in play. Before order was restored, the bell sounded signifying that the innings had been declared closed at 790–3. My innings had taken 10 hours 8 minutes against Hutton's 13 hours 20 minutes. Wisden said I hit 38 fours and did not mention any sixes. I cannot remember if I hit any sixes. I find that rather strange! I hit many balls out of the ground at Sabina Park in my time. It was my favourite scoring ground.

When the pitch was eventually cleared, the wily Kardar pointed to a couple of indentations in the pitch and claimed it would be unfair for his team to start their innings on a damaged surface. The umpires agreed and the final fifty-five minutes of that day's play was cancelled.

That innings didn't change me as a person but it changed my life.

From that moment on, I was instantly recognised throughout the Caribbean and the cricketing world. It did not alter my bank balance. There were no bonuses in those days, just the 150 EC dollars match fee as I remember. We won the match by an innings and 174 runs early on the final morning.

One person who congratulated me, one of many hundreds, was Len Hutton. He said he was pleased for me and hoped I would break more records.

He was a few months older than me, twenty-two, when he set the record. I had seen him score 205 against us in Kingston three years earlier and knew from my own experience what a fine player he was, even though he was past his best. I would have no hesitation in calling him a great player. He was strong all round the wicket and, though some critics said he was uncomfortable against extreme pace and wasn't a hooker, he played short-pitched bowling as well as anyone I knew.

He went back and played it down in front of him. He wasn't frightened of it. England had an indifferent batting side just after the war, and there were times when he carried the innings almost singlehandedly. I was proud to have beaten his record.

8 | A Late Night at Lord's

One of my most satisfying innings was the 150 not out in my final Test appearance at Lord's in 1973. But what most of the 25,000 crowd didn't know was that I failed to go to bed on the Thursday night! It was well known in cricket that I liked a drink after play. I rarely went to bed at a normal time because I am one of those people who can have four or five hours' sleep and still wake up fresh.

Instead of lying in bed thinking over what had happened on the field of play, I preferred to go out with friends to restaurants and clubs. My philosophy was, and still is, that life is for living. I played hard and drank reasonably hard on occasions without making a fool of myself.

I enjoyed the social side of cricket so much that it was to become my motivation to do well. If I were to have a bad run with the bat, people would start asking questions and might come up with the answer that my failure was due to too many late nights. I had to make sure those late nights could continue by maintaining a consistently high level of performance.

Many cricketers liked a night out during matches. It was a traditional part of the game, particularly when Australians were involved. Not that all Australian cricketers were like that. Some, like Brian Booth, Ken 'Slasher' Mackay and Neil Harvey, didn't drink at all, although I believe Ken and Neil did when they retired. Nowadays, with cricket becoming much more competitive and the rewards for success greater, there are fewer opportunities for players to enjoy themselves after hours. Most teams have curfews, and anyone staying out will soon find himself in trouble.

My 'live for today' approach was really fostered by the late Sir Frank Worrell. He liked to enjoy himself after matches, and I remember many nights when we sat up together in hotels talking and drinking. There was a curfew for the team, but he used to say to me: 'That's not for you. I know you well enough.'

What he meant was that he recognised we had a lot in common. He knew that if I went to bed early I wouldn't sleep. My view about sleep is that you go to bed when you are tired. If you still have plenty of energy to burn, you burn it.

After close of play on the Friday of the Lord's Test, I met an old friend of mine now living in London, Reg Scarlett, the former Jamaican and West Indian off-spin bowler. Reg was a useful player and should have played more than the three Tests he was picked for against England in 1959. We were out until 5 a.m. and then went back to the hotel where we never managed to get any sleep!

Reg drove me to the ground in the morning, and I resumed my innings. The West Indies were in a very strong position. Skipper Rohan Kanhai, timing the ball superbly, made 157, and Bernard Julien helped me add 231 for the seventh wicket on one of the best Lord's batting pitches I ever encountered.

Wisden records that 'there was a quiet period at the start when Sobers played within himself'. That was probably because I wasn't seeing the ball too clearly! Bob Willis, then twenty-four and bowling at his fastest, beat me several times, and I remember saying to myself: Just play straight.

I managed to overcome the crisis, and when I was in the seventies felt churning pains in the stomach. They were so bad that I thought about going off. But I rejected that option because I felt it would break my concentration. I needed that twenty-sixth Test hundred to prove to the selectors who had left me out of the previous series against the Australians that I was still a good player!

When I eventually passed my hundred, the discomfort was such that I said to umpire Charlie Elliott: 'I'm not feeling well. Can I go off?' Charlie sounded a little perplexed. 'You're not injured,' he said. 'What can I put it down to?'

'I can't stay,' I said. 'I've got to go.' So off I went and in came Keith Boyce to join Julien.

Around this time the authorities were still letting spectators sit on the grass at Lord's. There had been pitch invasions at the Oval, and they were followed by more at Lord's. So many people came on that it became tiresome, and the MCC finally decided to ban sitting on the grass. When Julien reached his hundred off 127 balls, on came several hundred fans, and umpire Dickie Bird was most upset but powerless to act.

This was also the Test where a bomb scare held up play on the Saturday. All these matters were far from my mind as I slumped on a chair in the dressing-room and Rohan Kanhai asked me what was wrong.

'Captain, I had to come off,' I said. 'My stomach is giving me trouble.' Even after he had taken over from me, Rohan always called me 'Captain' and, turning to the twelfth man, said: 'Bring the captain a brandy and port to settle his stomach.' The drink was quickly produced, and I drank it. Rohan knew that a brandy and port usually worked with me. As I downed it, Rohan said: 'Bring the captain another brandy and port.' So I had another one!

Boyce was eventually out for 36 at 604–7, and to my surprise Rohan asked me to resume my innings. I believe John Arlott was commentating at the time. 'Goodness me,' he said. 'West Indies 604 for 7 and here comes Sobers.' I will never forget the expression of sheer disbelief on the face of England captain Ray Illingworth when I walked out of the pavilion.

Rohan declared when I reached 150 with the total at 652–8. England, thoroughly demoralised, were bowled out for 233 and 193, and we won by an innings and 226, the second-biggest Test victory of all time up until then. The biggest was England's defeat in Brisbane in 1946–7. It was Illingworth's last Test as captain. Mike Denness, captain of Kent, took over for the tour to the West Indies later that year.

Another occasion when I did well after a night out was in Perth in 1968. I had a date and spent the night out of the hotel. When I arrived back the team was leaving and there wasn't time to catch up on any sleep. The West Indies were batting in reply to Western Australia's 199, and I was in my usual position of six. Just to make sure I would be ready when my turn came, I put my pads on and went to sleep.

Wickets fell quickly, and it wasn't long before one of the other players jogged my arm and said: 'You're in.'

'What's happening?' I said.

'Chap named Gannon has been taking a few wickets,' he replied.

'Who is he?' I said. 'Never heard of him.'

It was an innings when everything went off the middle of the bat, and I managed to score 132 in 113 minutes against an attack which included Test bowlers Graham McKenzie, Laurie Mayne, Tony Lock and Sam Gannon. When I was out, I returned to the dressing-room to continue my sleep!

This habit of mine of going out and having a drink was temporarily interrupted when I toured India for the first time in 1958–9. It was virtually impossible to get an alcoholic drink anywhere. As tourists, we were given an allowance of coupons to exchange for an odd bottle, but it did not amount to much between the whole team.

As Christmas approached in Kanpur in 1958 I said to Eric Atkinson, brother of Denis Atkinson, that we should try to beat the embargo. We found some upper-class people with access to a supply of whisky and agreed to meet them later to celebrate.

The team manager was Berkeley Gaskin, the former Guyanan bowler and administrator. I liked Berkeley. He had a sense of humour and did his best to be strict with the young players. Eric and I had our little night out, and it was around 2 a.m. when we returned to the hotel. No one was about, and we thought our mission had been undetected. Next day I went out and scored 198 in just over five hours before Joe Solomon ran me out. In the dressing-room, Berkeley was there to greet me. 'Good thing you got those runs,' he said. 'I saw you come in late!'

He was still a good enough bowler to help me out in the nets, and one day he bowled me out. He picked up his coat and walked off. 'That's it,' he said. 'My job is done.'

Earlier in my career I did not drink a lot. But then occurred an event in my life that changed that and for a time forced me to seek comfort from drink: the death of my great friend Collie Smith in a car crash in 1959.

O'Neil Gordon Smith, to give him his full name, was a League professional with me in Lancashire. He was three years older and potentially one of the most outstanding cricketers the Caribbean has ever produced. During the 1957 tour of England he showed his class with innings of 161 and 168 in Tests. In only his third game for Jamaica, he scored 169 against the Australians and went on to make 104 against them in his first Test.

We used to call him 'The Mighty Mouse' or 'The Wayside Preacher' because he liked reading the lesson in church. He was an admirer of the England opening batsman David Sheppard, who went into the Church and was to become the Bishop of Liverpool.

Collie shared a room with me in England and also in Pakistan, where his wise advice and support helped me overcome the shock of being umpired out three times in quick succession. He played for Burnley and I played for Radcliffe in the Lancashire League. In July of that year he created a League record by scoring 306 in the Burnley v. Lowerhouse match, a one-day game.

On the night of 6 September I picked him and Tom Dewdney up to travel through the night to a charity match the next day in London. We left it late because of the heavy traffic. Tom was a big Jamaican medium-fast bowler who played 9 Tests between 1955 and 1958.

I do not remember much about the accident. But at the inquest on Collie a few weeks later it was said that I was driving on the A34 near Stone in Staffordshire when my vehicle ran into a ten-ton cattle-truck driven by a Mr Andrew Saunders. The time of the collision was 4.45 a.m.

I remember being blinded by headlights as I approached a bend and was sure my car was on the right side of the road. The impact left us stunned, but none of us lost consciousness. Collie did not appear to be in too bad shape. 'Don't worry about me. Look after the big fellow,' he said, referring to Tom Dewdney.

We were taken to a hospital in Stone. I had a cut eye and a severed nerve in a finger on my left hand which took some time to mend. I was also suffering from shock. When I asked about Collie, the kind nurses and doctors said: 'Don't worry, he's coming along fine.' I learned that his spinal cord was damaged. Tom was recovering.

Three days later Collie died. I was stunned. He was such a wonderful person, such a good friend. He had the ability to become a better all-rounder than me. His off-spin bowling was in the Test class.

Collie provided the stabilising influence in my life up to then. He was not puritanical. He loved enjoying himself as much as I did, but if I showed signs of going too far he would say: 'That's enough for tonight. Let's go home.'

Around that time, with plenty of time to spare between weekend matches, I became increasingly interested in gambling on horses. It was something to do. Now, with Collie gone, I had no restraints. I drank heavily, I had the capacity to down a lot of liquor without it having any harmful effects on me.

Later I was charged with driving without due care and attention and was fined £10. It was the saddest episode of my life and it has been on my conscience ever since. Two weeks after the crash, we were both due to return home for the series against Australia.

Around this time I began to bet regularly on horses. Like most West Indians, I was used to gambling from when I was a boy. The racecourse in Bridgetown is open on most sides, and anyone can watch. I signed for the Lancashire League side Radcliffe as successor to Frank Worrell in 1958 and found I had little to do during the day. There were matches at the weekend and practice sessions in the evening. The rest of the time was my own.

To amuse myself, I used to bet on horses. With some other West Indian players in the League, I used to go to a betting shop in Manchester and listen to the races. I enjoyed it but would not describe myself as a compulsive gambler. Most days I had a flutter.

I wouldn't put large amounts on a horse. Like all gamblers, I won some and lost some. I would not have described myself as a real gambler, the man who will bide his time to make his killing. I studied the form, made my selection and if I won occasionally that was satisfying.

We also went to the races in England and played cricket against the jockeys, some of whom, like Lester Piggott, Geoff Lewis and Wally Swinburne, became my friends.

Most sportsmen are gamblers, particularly cricketers with time on their hands. I do not see any harm in it, providing they are not too reckless and do not allow it to ruin their lives.

One of my passions now is owning horses, and Wes Hall and I share the ownership of a two-year-old colt named Cruise Missile which won two of its first four races in Barbados. Watching him win is more satisfying than making a big score in cricket!

Cruise Missile is ridden by Wes's twenty-one-year-old son Sean. Wes was my partner in many betting exploits around the world when we were touring together. If one of us had no money, the other would lend him some to make a bet.

On a visit to Australia, Wes fancied a horse called Young Pedro in a trotting race. Young Pedro was 10–1, but Wes claimed he'd had a lot of good information about the horse and decided he would invest $200 on it. When he told Neil Dansie, his colleague at South Australia, Neil said: 'You must be crazy. The favourite is a sure thing. Put your money on it. Don't bother with Young Pedro.' Wes took his advice, and the result of the race was Young Pedro first, the favourite unplaced.

Next day Wes went looking for Neil. When they met, Neil held up his hands in mock protection. 'I'll pay you off in instalments,' he said. In England once, Wes and I were among the few punters ever to lose on the great English jumper Arkle. Wes had an accumulator going through the meeting, and if Arkle won, as everyone expected, stood to win £6000.

At the last fence Arkle was a couple of feet in the lead. He jumped so well that he was three yards ahead as he started the run in.

Instead of going on strongly, he allowed himself to be beaten by a short distance, and afterwards it was announced that he had broken a bone in his foot as he landed at the last fence.

Just our luck!

9 | The Tied Test in Brisbane

The best tour I went on was my first to Australia in 1960–1 under Frank Worrell. And the greatest Test match I played in was the First Test in Brisbane, which ended in a tie. The Australians have since been involved in another tie, against the Indians in Madras in 1986, and like our match it ended with one possible ball to be bowled.

The first tie came in the 498th Test; the second in the 1052nd. Our match was notable for its sportsmanship, good comradeship and humour.

Before the tour of Australia began, Frank Worrell called us together and laid down some rules. If you were not happy about a decision, he said, you would leave the crease without showing your displeasure. There was not one incident with umpires on the whole tour. And he also said there was to be no time-wasting. There wasn't. The incoming batsman had to pass the outgoing batsman on the field of play to make sure no time was lost.

He told us to play like true sportsmen, win, lose or draw. 'No cocky nonsense if we win,' he reminded us. If we lost, there would be no recriminations, only an appraisal of where we went wrong and what we should do about it next time.

Team spirit was fostered on the boat going out when Sonny Ramadhin, Rohan Kanhai, Tom Dewdney, Wes Hall and myself did physical training exercises on deck every morning after late nights drinking and singing to the piano accompaniment of the late Ernest Eytle, who was covering the tour for the BBC. The other members of the team, most of whom played in the Lancashire League, flew out later.

I remember when we docked being taken to the Palace Hotel in

Perth and being asked if I would like a beer. They brought a small glass, much smaller than the glasses we were used to drinking from at home. 'You call this a beer?' I asked my host. 'Man, we can down twenty of these!'

'That's great,' he said. 'Go ahead.'

A dozen or so glasses later I felt so tired that I went to my room and collapsed. I'd learned that Australian beer was somewhat stronger than what I was accustomed to at home!

Frank Worrell reminded us that he did not want us behaving badly in public. 'I don't mind what you do in your room but don't do it in public,' he said. He treated us like adults.

In our eagerness to impress him and the Australian public, we were bowled out for 96 in the opening match against Western Australia. That night he said that aggressive cricket was fine but it had to be mixed with discretion. Trying to hit balls wide of the off stump was helpful to the Australian slip cordon but not to our team. Being too rash has always been a failing in West Indies cricket. That is why team meetings and communication with the captain are so important. He has to instil the right attitude. It's called leadership.

My own form fluctuated in the early weeks. I opened with a century in Perth, but by the time we went east to Sydney the runs were no longer coming. Richie Benaud bowled me first ball in the match against New South Wales, which we lost by an innings, and the press opinion was that I couldn't read the Australian skipper's bowling.

That was nonsense.

I never had any trouble reading Richie's googlies or his renowned flipper. The ball that dismissed me was his leg-break, and it came between bat and pad. It was just too good a ball to get so early. I was looking glum when Frank Worrell brought a visitor into the dressing-room in Sydney, Sir Donald Bradman, the greatest batsman of all time. I hadn't noticed he was there until I felt someone put his hand on my head in playful fashion and say: 'Don't you worry, son. You'll get them at the right time.'

I next met Sir Don two weeks later on the first morning of the First Test at the Woolloongabba, known as the Gabba, ground in

Brisbane. He was there in his capacity as an Australian selector. 'I hope you're not going to disappoint me this time,' he said. Frank won the toss and decided to bat, and the West Indies were 42–2 when I walked in to join Conrad Hunte.

Both wickets had fallen to Alan Davidson, the strongly built Australian left-arm over-the-wicket bowler. Davo probably gave me more trouble than almost any other bowler. He wasn't fast – not as fast as Ray Lindwall or Keith Miller – but he was capable of moving the ball late. His best ball was the one that swung in the air from off to leg and went away off the pitch: the classic left-arm swing bowler's delivery. As an exponent of it myself, I appreciated it when I saw it bowled by a real expert. Being a left-hander, it was easier for me to play, but he also had the delivery that went straight on and the one that left you.

He was a great bowler who would have been just as successful today. None of the great Australian bowlers, including Dennis Lillee, Miller, Lindwall and Benaud, could equal his Test bowling average of 20.53. In the pre-Test matches, I was getting out early because I was taking Frank Worrell's words too literally. I was being too defensive.

I decided I would play my normal attacking game. Early on in my innings Ian Meckiff, another left-arm bowler, bowled me a slower delivery which I spooned up for a possible catch.

Luckily Richie Benaud did not have a fielder close enough to catch it. When Meckiff tried another slower ball I was ready. I was on the back foot and punched it straight out of the field into a bar. The commentators described it as 'an unorthodox but effective shot'. Being able to play a shot like that in a split second went back to the years of practising my own special brand of shots in Barbados.

The commentators talked about what would happen when Benaud finally put himself on to bowl. In his first over I went back, and he thought he had bowled me, so late did I play the ball. I drove it straight past him for four. That must have convinced the commentators that I had no worries about facing him. Richie's googly did not turn a lot, especially on a good batting pitch like the Gabba's was that day. He got many wickets with the 'flipper', his version of the top-spinner which skidded through quicker and lower.

When I was caught off a Meckiff full toss I had scored 132 in well under three hours. It was a 'sweet hand' as we used to say in Bay Land. Sir Don was one of the first people to come into the dressing-room. 'Congratulations,' he said. 'You didn't disappoint me.'

Our first innings 453 ought to have provided us with a lead, but I dropped Norman O'Neill at slip when he was 47 off Frank and Norm went on to score 181 in Australia's total of 505. Norm had a big reputation in the fifties. He was called the next Don Bradman but never succeeded in living up to all the forecasts. He was a good player, there was no doubt about that. His problem was his temperament. He used to be very nervous before going in to bat.

When I was playing Sheffield Shield cricket two years later he was going through a bad period, and I gave him a pep-talk before one particular match. Good players often need more reassurance than ordinary players. 'I can't understand it,' he said. 'I can't get a run.'

'That's because you're not playing your normal game,' I said. 'Your game is to play shots. That's your style. Go out there and hit the ball.'

He duly scored a hundred, which upset Ian McLachlan, my South Australian colleague who was twelfth man for Australia that year and was next in line to take his place.

Our second innings in Brisbane was less successful: 284, with Frank Worrell scoring 65, which he had done in the first innings as well. Davo was the problem. He bowled me for 14 and took 6–87 to add to his 5–135 in the first innings. Less than 4000 people were in the ground for the final day's play to see if Australia could reach their target of 233 in 310 minutes. The others must have thought it was going to end in a dull draw.

At no stage did we think the match was out of our grasp. Frank kept urging us on, convinced that we would win. Richie had the same attitude. Two great captains were of the same mind: that their side could win. Wes Hall, who invented the phrase 'pace like fire' around this time, was bowling at his fastest. Bobby Simpson was caught by the substitute, Lance Gibbs, for nought. I dived to catch

Neil Harvey, one of the great left-handers of Australian cricket, stubbing a finger into the ground and dislocating it as I did so.

Wicket-keeper Gerry Alexander, a veterinary surgeon, yanked the finger back into place and there was a lot of ribbing from the other players. Hall removed O'Neill after an hour, and Frank bowled the patient Colin McDonald. In came the late Les Favell, soon to be my skipper at South Australia. When he put me on to bowl, he would announce: 'We now have Sobey in his faster style,' or 'Sobey will now come on and bowl his slow left-hand Chinamen.'

Les didn't stay long, caught by little Joe Solomon off Hall. Five wickets were down for 57. The boys were getting excited. Ken 'Slasher' Mackay and Davo were together. The nickname 'Slasher' was a misnomer. Ken was a left-hander who could defend as well as Trevor Bailey. He was the game's most incessant gum-chewer. Sadly, he is dead. And so, too, is Les Favell.

These two took the score to 92 before Ramadhin bowled 'Slasher'. Australia 92–6, and Benaud and Davo were the last of the batsmen. Sometimes Frank would get flustered, and he must have been on this occasion but he never showed it. He kept his emotions bottled up, and his players took their mood from him.

It was difficult for them, because both Davo and Benaud passed their fifty. The 200 came up, and it seemed the Australians were going to be victors by 4 wickets. Just 7 were required when Davo tried a quick single and Solomon, one of the best throwers in the game, hit the stumps with only one to aim at. Davo out for 80. Australia 226–7.

When the last eight-ball over started, 6 runs were needed. A leg-bye came off the first ball, and Benaud, hooking at a short delivery from Wes, was caught behind for 52. Australia 228–8. In came Ian Meckiff, a non-batter, to join Grout. Wes was hopping up and down, and Frank told him: 'Whatever you do, don't bowl a no ball or they won't let you back into Barbados.'

A bye came off the fourth delivery. Off the fifth, Hall shouted 'Mine' when Grout mishit a catch towards square leg, only to drop it. One more run: 230–8.

The sixth ball was played behind square on the leg side by Meckiff, and Conrad Hunte set off after it. Conrad was not known as the team's best thrower from the boundary, but with the batsmen turning for a third his throw came right in over the stumps and a diving Grout was run out – 232–9 with two balls remaining.

Kline played the seventh ball to leg and scampered off down the pitch. Meckiff, fractionally hesitant, was beaten by Solomon's direct throw – the most famous run-out in history!

Kanhai jumped up and down. 'We've won, we've won,' he shouted. Several other players thought the same. The Australians congratulated us as we came off. 'It's a tie,' they said.

That incredible game set the tone for the rest of a wonderful tour. There were incidents all the time. In the second Test in Melbourne, Joe Solomon was given out hit wicket when his cap fell on the bails as he tried to pull Benaud. The crowd were so upset they booed Richie! We lost that game by 7 wickets, with me making 9 and 0 and Frank a pair.

In the Third Test in Sydney, which we won by 222 runs, Lance Gibbs took three wickets in four balls. I was 160 not out at the end of the first day, and Frank reminded me of how I had got out a few times by playing the hook shot. 'Garry, try to cut them out,' he said. Next morning, after a few deliveries, I tried to hook Davidson and was caught and bowled for 168!

Gibbs went one better in the Fourth Test and became the first bowler to take a hat trick in Adelaide, and Kanhai scored two brilliant hundreds in a drawn game. So it was on to Melbourne for the decider. So much interest had been created that a world-record crowd of 90,800 watched the second day's play. I had to be at my fittest to bowl 44 overs at my faster pace, taking 5–120. Australia needed 258 to win, and Bobby Simpson made sure that Wes Hall wouldn't stop them this time by hitting 18 off the first over. Simpson's 92 was the crucial innings.

The seventh wicket fell at 248, and we wondered whether another tie was looming. At 254–7 another strange incident occurred. Grout tried to cut a ball from Alf Valentine and appeared to dislodge a bail. The batsmen ran two as Alexander and Valentine pointed to the fallen bail and appealed. After consulting his umpire colleague, Col Egar ruled 'not out'. No one argued. The sporting Grout deliberately skied a catch to cover, Cammie Smith, in the next over and at 256–8 we might still have done it. Mackay, number eight in the order, and Johnny Martin saw that we didn't, and we lost the series 2–1.

As we left Melbourne, thousands of people turned out for a ticker-tape farewell. It was a proud moment for all of us. No team had ever had such a send-off, nor has had one since. It was the first trip to Australia for many of us and for me, like so many others, it was the start of a close association in the following years.

10 | Captain of the West Indies

By the time the West Indies next played the Australians, in 1965, I was captain and Sir Frank Worrell, knighted in 1964, was manager. I had never thought of being captain and I had no experience of the job, not even at club level. But I had served the best apprenticeship of all under Sir Frank and was confident I could do the job, especially with him at my side.

Before Sir Frank took over in 1960–1 in Australia, the practice was to give the job to amateurs of independent means like John Goddard, Gerry Alexander and Denis Atkinson. Sir Frank was the first black man to lead us; and Sir Learie Constantine, later Lord Constantine, said after Worrell led the West Indies to victory in England in 1963 that 'he changed the whole philosophy and structure of West Indies cricket'.

Conrad Hunte was vice-captain in England, and I thought he would succeed Frank when he retired. Conrad was popular, and there was no doubting that he was worth his place. But by the time the West Indies were preparing to take on Bobby Simpson's side in the Caribbean for the unofficial championship of the world Conrad was heavily involved in Moral Rearmament. The players liked him, but he had become somewhat remote from them. I believe that was the reason why he was overlooked.

I was playing for Norton, the North Staffordshire League side, when I received a letter in the 1964 season offering me the captaincy. It was some time before I could write back and accept. Perhaps I was slightly overwhelmed that someone with my humble background should be chosen.

At the end of that season I played a few matches for a West Indian team Sir Frank had assembled to play a series against an England side. In the final match at Lord's, Sir Frank came to me and said: 'Well, you'll be skipper of the West Indies from now on, so how about starting here?' It was the first time I had led a team on to the field, and it proved an almost meaningless exercise because there was only one day's play.

Sir Frank had retired with an outstanding record, winning nine Tests, drawing three and losing only two. I was to surpass him in only one respect: winning the toss. I managed to do so in 27 out of my 39 Tests, including my first Test on my favourite Test-match ground at Sabina Park.

The pitch was an extraordinary sight when Bobby Simpson and I went out to toss, bright and shining like a mirror. I knew it would have a lot of pace in it, and with Wes Hall and Charlie Griffith in their prime I was tempted to ask Australia to bat, but decided against it. Later on in my career, I would have had the confidence to insert the opposition. With so much attention on me in my first Test, I couldn't afford to gamble.

The Australians had no one of the pace of Wes or Charlie, who were the match-winning bowlers in our 2–1 victory, the first by the West Indies over an Australian team. The best Australian bowler was Neil Hawke, a well-liked character who bowled inswingers at a medium-fast pace.

Fast bowlers usually take the wickets in the Caribbean, but there have been a number of successful medium-pacers including Hawke, Bruce Taylor of New Zealand, Trevor Bailey and Hawke's successor Max Walker. Everyone called Hawke 'Hawk Eye', and after inspecting the mirror-like Sabina Park pitch he said: 'I think I'll bring my razor out and shave on that tomorrow.'

He was good at most sports – golf, Australian Rules football, table tennis and baseball. His most effective delivery was his 'knuckle ball', a slower ball which he picked up in baseball. A few years later when I was in Australia, I was shocked to hear that he was in hospital fighting for his life. I went to visit him, and he couldn't speak. He had to write things down on a piece of paper.

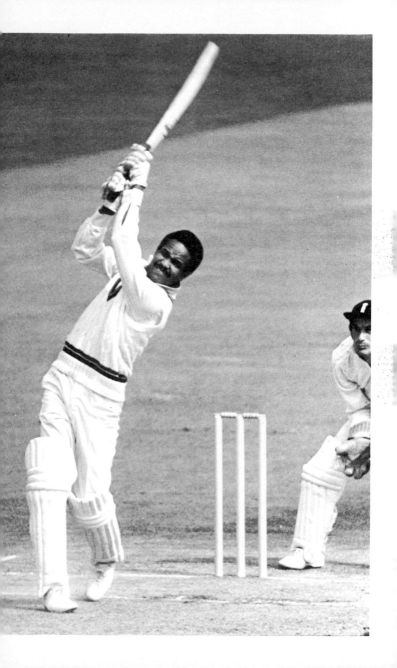

Facing up at the Bay Pasture, Barbados, where I first started playing cricket.

With my brother Gerry, who is a year older than me, outside our house in Walcott Avenue, Barbados. In those days it was made of wood; it has since been rebuilt in concrete on the original site.

Here I am looking bemused after being bowled by a fast delivery from Tony Lock, the England left-arm spin-bowler, MCC v. Barbados, 1954. Umpire Harold Walcott has raised his arm signalling a no-ball for throwing. In those days Lock had a reputation for throwing, but Fred Trueman, fielding at leg-slip, seems aggrieved at the decision.

...ning out to bat with my great mentor and inspiration, the late Sir Frank Worrell. Sir ...nk taught me about cricket and life, and it was a grievous blow to West Indies ...ket when he died at the early age of forty-three.

Celebrating at a cock[
party in Trinidad du[
the 1968 England T[
With me are (from l[
to right): Colin
Cowdrey; the late D[
Eric Williams, the P[
Minister of Trinidad
and Tobago; and,
looking over his
shoulder, Geoffrey
Boycott.

With Jeff Stollmeyer[
the team manager (l[
and Conrad Hunte,
vice-captain, I am
holding the Wisden
Trophy at the Wald[
Hotel in London as
captain of the West
Indies touring side.[
are in England to
defend the trophy in[
1966 Test series.

...lking off the field at Lord's in June 1966 after the match-winning stand with my ...usin David Holford. David, the cleverest of the family, went to Harrison College, one ...the island's best schools, and later got a degree at the University of the West Indies.

...captain of Notts, in June 1968. My team mates are: (back row, left to right) *Graham ...st, David Halfyard, Richard Bielby, Mike Smedley, Bob White, Mike Taylor;* (front ...w, left to right) *Carlton Forbes, Ian Moore, myself, Brian Bolus, Deryck Murray.*

Taking a sharp catch at second slip against India.

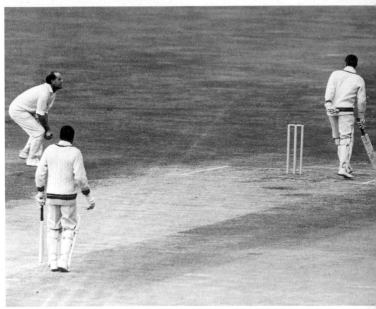

Caught out by England captain Brian Close at The Oval in 1966. John Snow, ordered
to bowl a bouncer, dropped the ball short. I played the ball a bit too early, edged on
my thigh, and Close, standing about five yards away, made an easy catch. Most fielde
seeing me shape to pull the ball, would have ducked out of the way.

What a way to finish your Test career! Bowled by a Derek Underwood full toss for 2 in the final Test against England at Port of Spain in 1974. I tried to place the ball between two fielders and in my anxiety played across the line.

But he was such a strong man, both in body and in spirit, that he pulled through.

He was the top wicket-taker in the series with 24 wickets, and Bob Cowper was the highest scorer with 417 runs. The left-handed Cowper was such a good player I thought he should have followed Simpson and taken over the captaincy. He retired after only 27 Tests and became very successful in business, with a house in Monte Carlo.

In the sixties many fine Australian cricketers retired too soon because they couldn't afford to play cricket as part-timers. Their wages from the Board were insufficient to compensate them for being away from their jobs. And they were away so long that their firms wouldn't pay them in their absence. It took the intervention of Kerry Packer to change that.

My fears about the Sabina Park pitch were soon confirmed. We were bowled out for 239 with Laurie Mayne, the third-string pace bowler, taking 4–43. Next day Wes bowled as fast as at any time in his career, and his 5–60 proved decisive. His match figures were 9–105, and we won by 179 runs. I achieved little myself, chiefly because of a strained thigh muscle, but I did manage to take my hundredth Test wicket when I had the Australian all-rounder Peter Philpott caught at leg slip by Rohan Kanhai.

Richie Benaud, by now a newspaper correspondent, angered the West Indian supporters when an article was published under his name during the match claiming that Charlie Griffith was a chucker. It was illustrated by a number of pictures. I do not know whether Richie's action was part of a plot by the visitors to discredit one of our match-winning bowlers, but it did not have the intended result because Charlie, used to criticism by that time, got on with his job in an even more determined way than ever. The criticism made him more hostile, and I am sure the campaign against him helped to motivate him.

When the tour was over Norman O'Neill wrote in a book that Charlie was a thrower, and the West Indies Board were so annoyed that they wrote to the Australian Board demanding an apology.

The Second Test was an uneventful draw, and the Third, in

Georgetown, was marred by a pre-match row over the umpires. The Guyanese umpires' association objected to the appointment of Cortez Jordan of Barbados, insisting that another local man be appointed to stand with their own Cec Kippins. Gerry Gomez, the former West Indies all-rounder and selector, replaced Jordan. Though he had not umpired a first-class match before, Gerry was a qualified umpire. He did an excellent job, even insisting that the creases should be remarked, delaying the start by a few minutes.

Spin proved more effective than pace, and with Lance Gibbs taking 9–80 in the match we won by 212 runs. Needing 357 to win, the Australians were 80–1 when I made a crucial decision which changed the course of the game. Gibbs was bowling into a stiff breeze, and he wanted my end. I agreed with him, and in the final session he bowled Bill Lawry, never an easy man to dismiss, had Cowper stumped and removed O'Neill, Brian Booth and Philpott, O'Neill and Philpott to catches by me in my close-up leg-slip position.

We won the rubber after an unsatisfactory draw in the Fourth Test in Bridgetown. I have always deplored time-wasting and gamesmanship, and we were the victims of it in the second innings. Simpson batted halfway into the third day before declaring at 650–6 after he and Lawry had put on 382 for the first wicket. We responded with 573, Seymour Nurse making 201 after Conrad Hunte retired temporarily following a blow in the face from a short ball delivered by McKenzie.

Batting a second time, the Australians declared at 175–4, setting us a fair target of 253 in 267 minutes. Hunte (81) and the Trinidad opener Bryan Davis, who played for Glamorgan for a spell, hit 145 for the first wicket, and Simpson lost interest in going for victory, setting the field back and asking his bowlers to bowl well up outside the off stump.

Why he did this I never knew, because a draw was of no use to him in the series. He should have continued to attack. We were under pressure to score quickly, and he might have bowled us out. I showed my annoyance by my antics. I was prepared to take chances against a normal field in an effort to get a boundary, but I declined to do so for singles to a cordon of eight men on the boundary. In the past a West Indies side might have got themselves out playing rash shots in that situation. I was 34 not out at the end, and we finished 11 runs short at 242–5.

The Final Test in Port of Spain was played on an appalling pitch. The ball would either keep low or jump at the batsman's head, and we were bowled out for 224 and 131, with Conrad Hunte carrying his bat through the second innings with 60. As a front-foot player, Conrad was better suited to the conditions than most of us. Simpson (72) and Cowper (69) managed to survive against Charlie Griffith, whose 6–46 was his best return of the series, and the Australians won by 10 wickets.

I was bowled in the first innings by one of the most interesting bowlers I have ever played against, the slow left-arm Chinaman and googly bowler David Sincock. No one turned the ball more than Sincock, who was known in the team as 'Evil Dick'. I had first encountered him in Adelaide on a previous trip to Australia. We were due to face Lindsay Kline and Johnny Martin, bowlers of similar type, and asked him to bowl to us in the nets. None of us could read his googly.

The ball fizzed through the air, and you had to try to see which way it was spinning. The delivery which bowled me in Trinidad pitched well outside my leg stump and hit off. 'What happened?' I said, and wicket-keeper Wally Grout said: 'Evil's done it again!'

Unfortunately for him, 'Evil' didn't do it enough, for he played in only 3 Tests. His bowling was too erratic. A normal over would be two or three full tosses, the same number of short ones and an unplayable delivery. As a practitioner of the art myself, I knew how difficult it was to bowl a length. It required constant practice. To be successful, you have to push the ball through, and length suffers. Tommy Greenhough, a right-hander, found that trouble in England and, though Johnny Wardle could bowl well in that style, there have been few other English masters of it.

Most of the better unorthodox left-hand bowlers come from Australia where the pitches suit them. Two of the best were George Tribe, who used to bowl with an arm which came from behind his back, and Jack Walsh. Today's batsmen would struggle against these two! It is a pity that the game doesn't have this type of bowler – a player who makes for more exciting cricket.

I nearly failed to go on the next visit to Australia, in 1968–9 when Bill Lawry had succeeded Simpson as the Australian captain. It was the closest I had come to resigning as captain. At the selection committee meeting to pick the party, the other selectors agreed that Wes Hall should be excluded. There was no other fast bowler in the West Indies in his class and, although I conceded Wes was past his best, I knew there was no one better. Wes was twenty-nine, and I felt he had at least one more tour left.

The selectors were adamant: no Hall. I was just as adamant. 'If Wes doesn't go, gentlemen, then I don't go,' I said. They were taken aback. After a short discussion, they decided that Wes should be picked. The short crisis was over.

I knew we would have problems defending the Frank Worrell Trophy, because the average age of the squad was twenty-nine. Charlie was nearing the end, too, and the only other fast bowler was the Barbadian Richard Edwards, known as 'Prof'. He played in two Tests and was expensive but, as I tried to explain to the selectors later, he was one of the chief victims of the spate of dropped catches. We dropped 34 in the series, which must be a record. One statistician said the count was 34 against 10, which was the main reason why we lost the series 3–1.

'Prof' was to prove in New Zealand later that he was a Test-class bowler, but he was left out of the tour of England in 1969 and never played again. That was yet another mistake made by the West Indian selectors.

Instead, they selected Pascall Roberts, a thirty-one-year-old bowler who was never going to become a Test bowler, and Philbert Blair, an equally unlikely choice. After opening the bowling in the first innings in the First Test in Brisbane, I reverted to orthodox slow left hand in the second innings and captured 6–73 in 33.6 overs, including Ian Chappell who cut a ball so hard it hit gully on the knee and rebounded to the substitute at point.

Chappell made up for that with 165 in the Second Test in

Melbourne which ended in victory for the Australians by an innings and 30 runs. By this time I was under attack in the press for going off and leaving the team to play golf or see my wife-to-be. Whenever I had done this in the past and we had won, nothing was said. Now it was seen as the major reason for our failure.

The depressing sequence of dropped catches continued in Sydney where we lost by 10 wickets. Most of our batsmen had trouble reading the bowling of Johnny Gleeson, the Australian bowler who spun the ball out of his hand with his middle finger. Basil Butcher claimed he could, only to cause a lot of laughter when he played for the off-break and found himself being caught in the covers off the one that went the other way.

There was dissension among the touring selectors. They wanted David Holford dropped and replaced by Charlie Davis, and I was overruled. That didn't help things.

We had 26 balls left to win the Fourth Test in Adelaide, a high-scoring match in which I returned to form with 110 in two hours. Australia needed 360 in five and three-quarter hours on the last day, and when 6 wickets fell for 29 runs leaving them at 333–9 I thought we might just do it. But Paul Sheahan and Alan Connolly survived.

This was the match when Charlie Griffith caused a row by running out Ian Redpath while backing up. Charlie hadn't warned him, and it caused a lot of bitterness. I never ran anyone out backing up because I didn't believe that was part of cricket. Yet it is permissible under the laws. Charlie probably did it on the spur of the moment. Several batsmen had been taking liberties, and Ian Chappell had previously been warned by David Holford. Redpath was caught in the same embarrassing position by Wes Hall in the Final Test, and Wes didn't run him out.

Someone suggested to the former Australian bowler Bill O'Reilly, sitting in the press-box, that he never resorted to such tactics, and Bill replied: 'When I was bowling, they weren't so anxious to get down the other end!'

Lawry's meanness as a captain was demonstrated in the final Test in Sydney when he batted on to 394–8 in the Australian second innings after gaining a first-innings lead of 340. That left the West

Indies a mammoth total of 735 to win, and we lost by 382 runs and, with it, the rubber. There were barely 300 people left in the ground at the end to see him presented with the Worrell Trophy. I was not surprised. Declarations like that drive the crowds away.

Most of us would have liked to go straight home but we had to spend the next month in New Zealand drawing a three-match series 1–1. The only two players who came out of the visit with any credit were Seymour Nurse, who said farewell to Test cricket with 558 runs, average 111, and 'Prof' Edwards, whose 15 wickets cost 23 apiece. 'Prof' bowled well in conditions that suited him more than in Australia.

In 7 Tests I played in New Zealand in my career, I averaged a mere 15. It was a great country to visit as long as you were not playing cricket!

11 | Charlie Griffith and the Chucking Row

Charlie Griffith was one of the greatest fast bowlers ever produced in the West Indies and one of the most abused. When he went to England in 1963 he was unfairly persecuted by many people, including a number of top-class cricketers and the press. They claimed he threw the occasional delivery, yet he had only been no-balled once for throwing at that stage of his career. I played with and against Charlie for many years and I never saw him throw. Cameras followed him around wherever he went, and they couldn't produce any documentary evidence to say he bowled illegally.

They said he threw his yorker, the ball which gave him so many of his wickets. I know that delivery of his was a genuine yorker. It was not thrown. Charlie made opposing batsmen think there might be something wrong with his action because he changed his pace cleverly. The quicker, well pitched-up delivery would be on to them before they expected it.

There is nothing unusual about a bowler disguising a change of pace. Most good bowlers are capable of doing it. One of the best in my time was the Australian Neil Hawke. He always had the batsmen thinking hard. A modern bowler who unsettles opponents by his change of pace is Michael Holding, and no one has complained about Michael's action.

Charlie was twenty-four when he arrived in England in 1963. It was his first visit abroad. A shy quiet-spoken person, he was forced to withdraw within himself by the attentions of the press. They treated him as if he was a tiger waiting to pounce, and it gave him the reputation of being surly, a Sonny Liston figure.

We knew that wasn't the real Charlie. Although diffident in those days, he wasn't unfriendly. He preferred to keep to himself and, rooming as he usually did with his talkative fast-bowling colleague Wes Hall, rarely had a chance to say very much. The public saw him as a silent menacing figure who had come to England to knock over their best batsmen by using illegal means. Charlie finished the tour with 119 wickets at an average of 12.83, an amazing return for a relatively inexperienced bowler on his first tour. But he wasn't able to convince the British public that he was a true sportsman. The doubts remained.

One of a family of eight from St Lucy, in the north of Barbados, Charlie was a wicket-keeper batsman at school. Then he played club cricket as an off-spinner before the absence of a fast bowler at his club, Lancaster, persuaded him to take up fast bowling.

Empire, the club that produced Everton Weekes, Seymour Nurse and Conrad Hunte, recruited him and, helped by Weekes, he developed so quickly that by the age of twenty-one he had dismissed three England captains, Colin Cowdrey, Mike Smith and Peter May, in the space of two overs for Barbados against the MCC on New Year's Eve, 1959.

The next day he sent yet another England captain, Ted Dexter, back to the pavilion and also Ken Barrington. When people talk of the resurgence of English cricket these days, I am reminded of the class of batsman they had in those days. The present team under Mike Gatting does not have players of this calibre, and bowling performances against England have to be assessed in that context.

So for Charlie to take those wickets at Kensington Oval was a wonderful achievement. Three years were to go by before he made his Test début. In the mean time there was the Nari Contractor affair in Bridgetown in March 1962. Nari was the Indian captain, a useful opening batsman leading a side which had beaten England not long before.

The match was Barbados versus the Indians, and Charlie opened the bowling with Wes Hall. Backing them up was another quick bowler, the engaging George Rock, one of cricket's characters. Contractor had scored 2 when Charlie bowled him a delivery, not far short of a length, which didn't get up.

Contractor, a left-hander, took his eye off the ball and tried to turn his head away from it as he ducked. It caught him above the right ear, and the noise was like hearing eggshells cracking. I was at first slip. It was a horrific moment. We rushed towards him as he lay on the ground, and I feared he might be dead. There was no 'kiss of life' in those days. Fortunately, the medical people were soon on the scene and Nari was helped off the field and on to hospital, about two miles away, where he underwent an emergency operation. The ball was low enough for us to justify an appeal for lbw, but no one appealed.

Charlie was crestfallen, but we told him it was not his fault. It hadn't been a bouncer, and Nari caused the problem for himself by the way he attempted to evade it. The first operation saved Nari's life, but there were complications. A blood clot formed, and a brain surgeon was flown in from Port of Spain to perform a second operation. Three of Nari's team mates, Chandra Borde, Bapu Nadkarni and Polly Umrigar, gave blood and so did Frank Worrell.

Nari had a steel plate inserted in his head and, though he played a little cricket later on, wearing a cork helmet, he was never the same player. That was the closest I had seen anyone come to losing their life on the cricket-field.

Another occasion when a batsman was hurt was on the same ground three years later, in my first season as West Indies captain. The player was Jackie Hendriks, in my view the finest wicket-keeper the West Indies have had, and this time the bowler was the Australian Graham McKenzie.

McKenzie bowled a short delivery, and Jackie, jumping to play it down, was struck on the side of the head and collapsed. His legs started to kick out as he lay on the pitch, and we feared that he might be seriously injured. He went to hospital and was released after a couple of days. Jackie knocked the wicket down as he fell, but Simpson declined to appeal. Bobby was a tough captain and a sporting one. That was the Test where Bill Lawry and Bobby

Simpson both scored double centuries in the same innings, the first time that had happened in Test cricket.

McKenzie was a useful bowler with a beautiful action, and his physique was ideal for a fast bowler. He was like Fred Trueman, broad-shouldered and thick in the thighs. With such a build, he should have been able to generate much more pace than he did, but his record of 246 Test wickets from 60 Tests was still a reasonable return for one of the leading Australian bowlers of postwar years.

Charlie played in that match and, frustrated at not being able to take a wicket, he conceded 169 runs and was warned for excessive use of the bouncer by umpire Cecil Kippins. Charlie bowled a well-directed bouncer. It pitched off stump, not all that short, and if the batsman moved into line to hook it he was looking right down the nozzle. It took a brave man to hook Charlie.

He was an intelligent bowler as well as a hostile one, and his partnership with Wes Hall was one of the best in the history of fast bowling. In the same match that Contractor was felled, Charlie also hit Vijay Manjrekar on the nose and forced him to retire. The Indians made only 86 and, with Contractor, Umrigar and Prasanna all missing in the second innings, lost by an innings and 95 runs. Manjrekar came back to score an unbeaten 100 in the second innings. He was a gutsy player and a stylish one, too.

The Indians, who went on to lose the series 5–0, must have been relieved that Charlie wasn't selected for the Tests. Before the series began, I played in a match against them with Seymour Nurse in Trinidad, and one night we were talking about fast bowlers. 'You haven't seen anything yet,' said Seymour. 'We've got one in Barbados called Charlie Griffith. He's frightening.'

They may have recalled that conversation later in the Bridgetown match! Nari's accident overshadowed another incident in that match when Charlie was no-balled for throwing by Cortez Jordan, the leading West Indian umpire at the time. That one ball plagued Charlie for the rest of his career. Whether it was justified it is not for me to say. I cannot remember that particular delivery.

It was one of roughly 20,000 deliveries that Charlie bowled in first-class cricket. How unfair to be judged on one offence! Not until May 1966 was Charlie to infringe again when English umpire Arthur Fagg no-balled him for throwing in a match against Lancashire at Old Trafford. I was resting in that match, so I did not see the incident.

The weather was bad, and neither side completed an innings. Fagg no-balled Charlie eight times for overstepping, and I am told that hardly anyone inside the ground realised that a ninth call had been for throwing. The incident was not reported in the newspapers or on the radio. But the next day the news came out, and we wondered how it had leaked if the correspondents who were present at the time knew nothing about it.

There was only one occasion on that 1966 tour of England when I had to take action to cool Charlie down and that was in Hove in June when we lost our first match of the tour to Sussex on a green pitch. John Snow took 11 wickets, and we were bowled out for 67 in the second innings – nine more than the lowest ever score by a West Indian side in England.

The players were upset because they felt the pitch had been deliberately prepared to suit the Sussex medium-pacers. In those conditions, when the ball is seaming around, the medium-pace bowlers are more damaging than quick bowlers.

Sussex needed only 6 to win in their second innings, and Charlie was fuming. 'If they can give us a pitch like that, let's see how they like batting on it,' he said. He was always a fiercely determined competitor, and it didn't matter to him that 6 runs only were required.

Charlie's first ball was frighteningly quick and struck the Sussex left-hander Ken Suttle on the jaw. Suttle retired to hospital for an X-ray, which showed no damage. In the same over, Charlie had Peter Graves, a twenty-year-old who made 64 in the first innings, leg before for 0. Most of his deliveries were short and extremely menacing. I told him to have a rest at the end of the over. There was no point stirring up more trouble for ourselves.

Later on in his career Charlie was more mature and could handle the problems better. But he still couldn't come to terms with being hounded all the time. He joined Burnley as their professional in the

Lancashire League and was popular on and off the field. He was highly successful. Some of the batsmen in the League played him with more resolution than county players.

In the late fifties there had been a campaign against bowlers who threw the ball, and perhaps Charlie caught the tail end of it. In Australia, Sir Don Bradman took the lead in persuading the authorities to eliminate offenders for the good of cricket.

Bowlers like Jim Burke and Keith Slater were self-confessed chuckers, and the English were unhappy with the bowling of Ian Meckiff and Gordon Rorke when they lost in 1958–9. By the time I played against Meckiff later I did not think he was infringing. He retired shortly afterwards.

Rorke's chief offence was dragging. By the time he released the ball, he was several yards down the wicket, which made him an awkward proposition. England, too, had chuckers, notably the Surrey pair Peter Loader and Tony Lock.

I remember playing against Lock in Bridgetown, and he bowled me with the quicker ball while my bat was still on the back lift. Only an illegal delivery could have done that, because the ball came through so much faster. Later, in the West Indies, Lock was no-balled by umpire Harold Walcott, uncle of Clyde Walcott, for throwing and remodelled his action.

When I next played against him, he said: 'What I am doing now is bowling. I don't know what I was doing before.'

The controversy about Charlie's action erupted again on the third day of the Lord's Test in 1966. One of the newspapers carried extracts from a book called *Ted Dexter Declares*, and in the article Ted revived the familiar story about Nari Contractor and how Charlie had been no-balled.

Ted was an old friend of mine, but it was inexcusable that he should resurrect the old arguments right in the middle of a Test match. Dexter relayed a conversation he alleged he had had with Contractor, who told him that he had been warned by the late Sir Frank Worrell about Griffith being a chucker. Sir Frank always denied the story.

The reawakened controversy had a bad effect on Charlie. That night he came to my hotel room and said he wanted to go home. As someone who packed his bags in Pakistan and wanted to do the same thing earlier in his career before seeing sense, I could understand how he was feeling. Underneath that inscrutable exterior, Charlie was a deeply sensitive man.

'These people are trying to destroy me,' he said. 'I can't ignore them. Cricket is my living, and they're trying to take my bread away. All the time I've been hoping things would quieten down, but they've just got worse. I think I ought to pack my bags and go home. Maybe that would be best for me and for the team.'

I told Charlie about my experiences in Pakistan when I felt just as exasperated. 'You just keep your mind fixed on those men in white coats,' I said. 'If they say nothing about your action, you're OK.'

He accepted my advice. 'Better get some sleep,' he said. 'There's a heavy day tomorrow.'

Charlie was only warned once in that series – on the third day of the Fourth Test at Headingley, which the West Indies won by an innings and 55 runs to clinch the series. England were 18–2 when Charlie bowled a bouncer to Tom Graveney which Tom ducked under. At the end of the over umpire Charlie Elliott conferred with his fellow-umpire, Sid Buller, both men I respected as the top men in their business, and Elliott said to Charlie: 'You can bowl, Charlie, but any more like that one and I will have to call you. That delivery to Graveney looked funny.'

Wisden was to record later that it was 'a vicious bouncer'. Charlie was very upset. He came to me and said: 'The umpire is being influenced by the England players. When I bowled that one I saw the batsmen turning to him as if they were saying: "What about that one?"'

I believed he had some justification for saying that, and went to Elliott and told him: 'Was that your decision or did you make it because of the England players?'

Elliott replied: 'It was my decision, Garry, and mine alone. I just didn't like the way he bowled that short ball.'

Charlie carried on bowling, and far from being crestfallen, he bowled even faster, althoug he took only one more wicket in the match.

Charlie had been strongly criticised in the press during the previous Test at Trent Bridge. This time his offence was bowling a bouncer at Derek Underwood, England's last man, which hit him in the face as he tried to avoid it. Underwood tumbled to the ground, and on television the experts condemned Charlie for turning away and not going to Underwood.

What happened was that Underwood did not go down straight away. He stood with his arm across his face for a split second, and Charlie thought the ball had only hit him on the arm. As soon as Charlie realised there had been contact with his face, he ran to him and apologised.

I did not agree with bowling a bouncer at a number eleven, and told Charlie so, but I did not accept the view of some critics that it had been a deliberate act. Charlie never tried to hit anyone. The bouncer is an accepted part of the game. The bowler uses it to unsettle batsmen, and there has never been any question of banning it, only of keeping its use within acceptable limits.

Charlie felt he was entitled to try one on Underwood, because the Kent bowler had batted for eighty-five minutes in the first innings and helped Basil d'Oliveira add 65 valuable runs for the last wicket. Underwood was proving just as obstinate in the second innings. He was able to bat on and was 10 not out when England's final wicket fell.

Underwood never complained about it himself and he accepted Charlie's apology when he wrote to him later. But even that gesture by Charlie was distorted. It was said that I had ordered him to write it, which was untrue.

Charlie loved bowling and he enjoyed bowling fast to batsmen who could bat. He wanted to pit his wits against theirs. He was a dangerous and feared opponent, but he never did more than the job of any talented fast bowler – to try to get batsmen out as quickly as possible.

He was a fitness fanatic on his tours abroad and he still is in his late forties. He was physical training instructor to the Barbados team and used to complain that he would do more of the exercises than the players who were half his age. A bachelor, he looks fitter now than when he was playing.

Charlie still plays over-forties cricket and, though naturally his fearsome pace has gone, he's the bowler they all watch out for and respect.

12 | Frank's Last Tour – England, 1963

At one time there was a possibility that I might not have been available for the 1963 tour of England, the tour that confirmed Frank Worrell's side as the top team in world cricket. I was playing for South Australia in Melbourne when the West Indies Board of Control invited me to be a member of the touring party.

I was elated to be asked, but not so happy about the pay being offered. If I remember rightly, it was in the region of £800, less than I could make playing League cricket one day a week. It was a full tour, and I could expect to be playing six days a week. I played in twenty-four matches, more than anyone else in the party.

These were the days before 'man of the match' awards, win bonuses and other perks which are commonplace today. Our expenses were paid, and there was a small daily allowance, but I did not think it was enough; and Wes Hall, who was playing for Queensland at the time, agreed with me. Neither of us replied to the letter, and eventually it came out in the press. We were criticised, as sportsmen usually are in these circumstances.

One of the first people I spoke to about my dilemma was Sir Donald Bradman. He told me: 'I think you are being underpaid for your ability. With your standing in cricket, you should get more money than anyone in the game. But I really cannot look at it in this way. You might ask for lots of money and you go there and fail. I don't say you will, but it can happen. Then everyone will say: "You wanted all this money and now you fail us."'

'But what if I do well?' I asked.

'So you might,' he said. 'I'm sure you will, but you cannot prove it right now. My advice is for you to go to England on these terms, because this is not the end but perhaps a beginning of something else for you.'

Richie Benaud gave me similar advice. 'I think you are the world's greatest all-rounder. But, putting that aside, I think you should go to England.'

I had not finally made up my mind when I received a letter from Frank Worrell. It was strongly worded. He said I should go and not worry about money. I should be more concerned about representing my country. I knew he was right and cabled my acceptance to the Board.

These days the Board have a scheme which guarantees experienced players extra sums for the tours they have undertaken in the past, so they are paid more than newcomers. It is a fairer system. West Indies cricketers are now among the best paid in the world, as they deserve to be.

Frank Worrell's side was one of the best-balanced Test teams of all time: strong batting (Conrad Hunte, Rohan Kanhai, Seymour Nurse, Basil Butcher, Joe Solomon, myself and Frank Worrell), a varied attack (Wes Hall and Charlie to open, myself first change and Frank, medium pace, and Lance Gibbs, off-spin), plus a promising young wicket-keeper in Deryck Murray who took over from David Allen when Allen went down with influenza.

Early in the tour, Trinidadian leg-spinner Willie Rodriguez went down with a cartilage operation and Tony White was called on to replace him.

Willie, one of the leading footballers in the Caribbean, made a swift recovery, which meant we had eighteen players in the party, rather more than Frank Worrell needed because he was insisting on a rota system to give everyone a game.

One of Frank's first acts was to ban the playing of cards when we were off the field because of poor weather. There is so much time to fill on cricket tours that card-playing is an essential feature. Frank even asked us to cut down on our evening bridge sessions.

He had studied optics and believed that playing cards in dim light had an adverse effect on the eyes of sportsmen. He reasoned that a batsman could get out through mistiming a stroke because his eyesight hadn't adjusted, or a fielder could drop a vital catch. It was the first time in my experience anyone had raised the subject, and it showed how deeply he was thinking about the team's wellbeing and success.

So we switched to table tennis wherever we could find a table. I had played a lot of table tennis in Barbados and found it a fine game for sharpening reflexes and keeping muscles in good shape. We filled our off-duty hours reading, listening to music, having an occasional drink and discussing cricket.

Young players learn from these sessions when the older players talk about cricket, and I believe the game has suffered because not so much of it goes on these days because of tighter schedules and less opportunity to get together.

It was a typically wet and cold start to the summer. The opening match against Worcestershire was wrecked by rain, and in the second game against Gloucestershire we were bowled out for 89. This was the first experience some of the newcomers had of a high-class English medium-pace bowler operating in favourable conditions. The bowler was Dave Smith, who had match figures of 11–92. Charlie Griffith was even more devastating with 8–23 in the first innings and 5–35 in the second, and we won by 65 runs.

In those days Yorkshire had the leading side in England. They were champions, and only two of the team that beat us at Middlesbrough were not experienced England internationals. Fred Trueman was then in his prime, and his figures of 10–81 bowled us to defeat. When overseas players were admitted to the county championship in 1968, Yorkshire's fortunes declined, but a restriction of one overseas player per county has helped them retain some of their status in recent years.

The First Test that year was at Old Trafford, where the pitch has always aided spin bowlers. Jim Laker was immortalised there, and on this tour our off-spinner Lance Gibbs was the bowler who did the damage with 11–157. The mainstay of our only innings (501–6) was Conrad Hunte, whose 182 occupied eight hours. Our

ten-wicket victory was our sixth successive Test victory, a record
for the West Indies.

One of the few English batsmen to hold us up was Micky Stewart,
the present England manager, who made 87 in the second innings.
The England selectors were relying on him to make an all-Surrey
opening partnership with John Edrich, a gutsy player who was a
proven Test batsman.

Micky was never quite able to fulfil his promise. He had a good
record against fast bowling but was rarely able to get on top of the
bowling of Wes and Charlie. He played four Tests in that series, and
his brief international career ended after eight appearances.

The Second Test at Lord's was labelled one of the most dramatic
matches ever played at the old ground. When the final over was due,
there were four possible results: a win for either side, a tie or a draw.
It was bowled, as in the tied Test in Brisbane, by Wes Hall, and 8
runs were needed. Wes had been bowling since play started at 2.20,
flat out for 3 hours 20 minutes. It was a phenomenal effort by a
great bowler. He was running in just as fast in his final over, his
fortieth, as he was in his first.

A single off the second ball and another off the third brought the
Hampshire veteran Derek Shackleton to take strike. Grey-haired
and looking like a schoolmaster, Shackleton was playing in his last
Test series at the age of thirty-eight after starting his brief, interrupted international career thirteen years earlier. He made one
appearance against the West Indies in 1950, one against South
Africa in 1951 and one against India the same year. And he hadn't
played again until we arrived.

That was amazing, because he was one of the greatest medium-
pace bowlers England has produced and it has produced many over
the years. Another one was Tom Cartwright, who also had a short
international career (5 Tests). Both bowlers were very accurate and
moved the ball late both ways. Shack usually cut it, and you didn't
know which way it would got until it left the pitch. Occasionally he
would stick in a seamer. His length and line never strayed, and it
was very difficult scoring against him. In that Lord's Test he bowled

84 overs at 2 runs an over. Both he and Cartwright would be magnificent bowlers to have in today's one-day cricket.

Wes Hall's fourth ball went through to wicket-keeper Deryck Murray, and Shackleton unwisely set off for a run. Murray's throw, wide of the stumps, was picked up by Frank Worrell, who was then aged thirty-eight, the same as Shackleton. Both men were born in August 1924. Worrell won the race and knocked off the bails.

Six runs were needed off the last two balls with Colin Cowdrey, arm in a sling after breaking a bone above the left wrist, resuming his innings to applause all the way round the half-filled ground. Lord's had been packed for the opening four days, but the bad weather which delayed the start had deterred people from coming on the final, most interesting day.

David Allen, the Gloucestershire off-spin bowler, had to face. If it had been Cowdrey, we were told he had intended to switch to a left-handed guard to avoid any possible damage to his left arm. Wes was steamed up. 'If he wants to be a hero, I'll show him something,' he said. Cowdrey did not have to face a single delivery. Allen blocked both balls and the game ended in a draw.

If Headingley helps the swing bowlers and Old Trafford is famous for aiding spin bowlers, Lord's is renowned for staging matches which fluctuate in an exciting manner. Fortunes ebbed and flowed in this match, and the West Indies needed a valiant second-innings 133 from Basil Butcher, a vastly underrated player, to pull us away from the defeat the bowling of Trueman (11–52) and Shackleton (7–165) had seemingly engineered.

England needed 234 in their second innings, about par for the conditions. Edrich, Stewart and Dexter went for 31 before one of Ken Barrington's typically pugnacious innings pulled it back their way. Twice Ken lofted Gibbs for sixes. He was known as a grafter but he was also a fine stroke-player.

When the final day's play finally began, England's target was 118 more runs with 7 wickets left. Cowdrey was already out of action after being hit by Hall. Brian Close was Barrington's partner, and these two lifted the total to 130–4. Close batted in a remarkable manner. When Wes pitched short, which was often, he would

advance down the pitch and frequently let the ball hit his unprotec-
ted body. The next day's newspapers carried pictures of the black
and blue bruises covering his body. It was an amazingly courageous
performance, which only Close would have attempted. Personally I
wondered what he had a bat in his hands for!

Barrington was caught behind off Griffith, who except for five
overs from Gibbs bowled unchanged at the other end to Hall, and
when Parks, Fred Titmus and Trueman went Close decided to
change his tactics. He started to swing the bat, trying to hit sixes,
and he, too, was caught behind by Murray. His 70 was his highest
Test score.

England's team was a very good one, better than the present side,
and they gave us a close run before we eventually won the series
3–1. They won the Third Test at Birmingham through the inspired
bowling of Trueman, whose 12–119 was his best Test analysis.
Fred was thirty-two at the time and not as quick as he had been on
his first tour of the West Indies nine years earlier. Experience had
made him a far better bowler, and he could still bowl the occasional
very quick delivery. In the second innings his 7–44 saw us dismissed
for a paltry 91.

Between 1955 and 1973 I never missed a Test for the West Indies,
and the closest I came was the Fourth Test at Headingley in 1963. I
had an unbroken attendance record, not because I trained any
harder than anyone else, but because I never ducked out of matches.
I had been troubled by a whitlow on one of the fingers of my right
hand and missed most of the preceding match against Middlesex
because of it. When we arrived in Leeds the whitlow came off and
the finger turned septic. The pain was unbearable, and I had my arm
in a sling.

Despite the agony, this was one match I did not want to miss. The
series was level at 1–1, and I was desperate to prove to the critics
that I could make a Test hundred in England. Rohan Kanhai and
myself had still to achieve this milestone, and the subject had been
mentioned a few times by poison-pen letter-writers.

On the morning of the match, it was decided to lance the infected
area in an attempt to remove the swelling. Afterwards, the finger

was still extremely sore and the doctor advised me not to play. In the dressing-room the players were discussing which part of me they would miss: Sobers the batsman, Sobers the change bowler, Sobers the spin bowler or Sobers the fielder. 'None of those,' said Frank Worrell. 'We will miss Sobers the man.' And, turning to me, he said: 'I want you to play.' I knew I had no alternative.

I was hoping we would field first so I could spend a few more hours before having to don a batting-glove, but Frank decided to bat and at 71–3 I found myself going to the crease to join Rohan Kanhai. Fortunately the pain was not as great as I had feared. The only time I felt it was when Trueman's deliveries jarred the bat.

Kanhai and I put on 143 and, though I reached my hundred, he failed by 8 runs, Tony Lock sneaking one under his bat. My 102 came in four hours, and the next ball after reaching three figures I was out in an abnormal way. I drove very hard on the front foot a yard on to the bowler's left, and the ball might well have hit my partner Joe Solomon if he hadn't skipped out of the way. By removing himself from the line, Joe enabled Lock to drive across and make a brilliant left-handed catch an inch from the ground. I scolded him about that!

There was a photograph published of Joe jumping out of the way to allow Lock the room. Charlie Griffith routed England, all out 174, and despite a lead of 223 Frank Worrell decided to bat again instead of enforcing the follow-on. The West Indies second-innings 229 came at one a minute, and the 30,000 crowd (Headingley was able to cater for many more spectators in those days) saw some exhilarating stroke-play on the Saturday.

When the innings ended, I thought we might benefit if I took the new ball and not Wes. I knew Micky Stewart was like one of his successors, Geoff Boycott, in that he did not relish the ball which swung in late. I knew we had to get our overs in as quickly as possible and, with my twelve-yard run against Wes's thirty yards, we could bowl an extra over or two.

Almost apologetically, I put the idea to Frank. 'You know,' he said, 'that is just what I was thinking.' I bowled the first over, and the fourth delivery was a perfect inswinger which bowled Micky.

That was a memorable day's cricket for those lucky enough to have been present. Sixteen wickets fell and 347 runs were scored. England succumbed just after lunch on the Monday, and we went to the final Test at the Oval needing to avoid defeat to win the series.

The West Indies duly won by 8 wickets with a day to spare. Conrad Hunte with 80 and 108 not out was the batting saviour, and Charlie Griffith (9–137) the bowling hero, and thousands of West Indians in the 25,350 crowd (the Oval was also bigger in those days) invaded the pitch at the end.

Predictably, Charlie was involved in yet another controversy. Some of England's batsmen had not been happy with his bowling, nor Wes's, because they had been knocked about a bit, and Sid Buller warned both bowlers on the opening day. Just before the close, Buller walked over to Worrell after Charlie had bowled two successive bouncers and said: 'Look, this can't go on. You will have to stop it, Skipper.'

Though Frank may not have agreed, he accepted Buller's argument with demur. Like the rest of us, he had tremendous admiration for him as an umpire.

Charlie, less diplomatic, tried to respond. 'I'm allowed two every over,' he said.

'No, you're not,' said Buller. 'You are not allowed any.'

As Charlie was bowling against Brian Bolus, an opening batsman at the time, that was a remarkable statement!

With Trueman out of action with a ricked ankle, the West Indies found the task of scoring 255 to win a simple one. We were world champions!

13 | My Best Tour – England, 1966

My best tour in terms of figures was when I returned to England in 1966 as skipper and the West Indies again won the series 3–1. I scored centuries in the First, Second and Fourth Tests and finished with 722 runs, average 103.14, higher than any other West Indian on a tour of England. I also captured 20 wickets in all three of my bowling styles and won the toss on all five occasions!

The nucleus of the 1963 team survived except that Seymour Nurse was a regular in place of Frank Worrell and David Holford filled the place of Joe Solomon. The Wes Hall–Charlie Griffith partnership remained, and both were still bowlers of the highest class.

Fred Trueman and Brian Statham had departed the scene for England, and the opening bowlers were John Snow, not as good as Trueman but a reasonable bowler nevertheless, and the Lancastrian Ken Higgs. Ken was medium-fast and moved the ball considerably. His persistent efforts were rewarded with 24 wickets, twice as many as the next man in the list, Snow.

The England batting averages were headed by two men who could have done so much more for English cricket if given the opportunity: Tom Graveney and Colin Milburn. Tom was the classic stylist, a player who could score runs against all classes of bowling. Yet for some peculiar reason there were two long gaps in his international career between 1951 and 1969.

Milburn's story was a tragic one. He was fearless against fast bowling as he showed in his unbeaten 126 in the Lord's Test. But for a road accident which cost him the sight of an eye, he would have played many more than 9 Tests and might well have changed the course of English cricket because he was a very fast scorer. He batted with Geoff Boycott on two occasions in that series, and it could have become a formidable pairing.

He was run out for 0 in the First Test at Old Trafford but more than made up for it with 94 in the second innings. It was a one-sided contest with the West Indies winning by an innings and 40 runs. Going in at number six, the position I favoured at this stage of my career since it enabled me to wind down after bowling, I made 161, and Conrad Hunte scored 135. As in the 1963 Test at Old Trafford, Lance Gibbs was the match-winner with 10–106 and, despite scoring 69 in the second innings, England captain Mike Smith was sacked as captain. I thought it was tough on Mike after having just returned from a successful tour of Australia.

That year was the first time I skippered on an overseas tour, and it seemed as though I could do nothing wrong. Before the start of each Test I called 'heads' and each time I won to the dismay of the three England captains confronting me: Mike Smith, then Colin Cowdrey followed by Brian Close, called in for the final Test at the Oval.

As I have already said, Lord's is renowned for staging Tests that see-saw, and the one in 1966 was an even more dramatic example than usual. Our first-innings 269 was not a good score. Higgs, with 6–91, exploited the conditions admirably. In England's innings, Tom Graveney made 96 and Jim Parks, a fine player, scored 91.

Tom had been recalled at the age of thirty-nine after a break of three years, and he showed the selectors what a mistake they had made by leaving him out. Forty minutes before lunch on the Monday, the West Indies were in a desperate position, 95–5 with Hunte, Carew, Kanhai, Butcher and Nurse all dismissed by Higgs and the Essex all-rounder Barry Knight. Our lead was 9 runs, and half the side was gone.

I was still in, and the critics were saying that this was one occasion when I must have regretted not going in higher in the order. The odds against us escaping must have been very high indeed. My partner was David Holford, a cousin of mine who has a degree. He was playing in his second Test, having made his début at Old

Trafford when he scored 32 and had bowling figures of 3–34. I knew that he was a good batsman, good enough to stay around despite all the pressure, and when he came in I thought I would try to reassure him.

The mental side of batting is most important. You can have all the ability but, if your temperament is suspect, you will never make a Test player. Confidence is vital, and that comes from being in form and being positive. That was why I never looked at the bowler after he had delivered the ball. If I did that, I might start thinking about what he would try next.

Remove fear and the batsman is in a much stronger position to do his work. So I went down the pitch towards David and said: 'Look at this pitch. It's just like Kensington Oval back home, isn't it? Do you really feel there is anybody who can get you out if you put your head down on this?' He nodded and went off to get on with the job. There were resemblances between the Lord's pitch and Kensington – they were both good batting pitches – but Lord's does have its peculiarities like the slope and a slight rise at the Nursery End which the authorities had tried to remove a few years earlier.

But what I meant was that it was no more difficult batting at Lord's than at Kensington, and David had scored plenty of runs in his career. I was confident that he could stay with me. His temperament was ideal. He is a very calm, orderly person, and I knew the crowd would not affect him. Nor did the England fielders, crowding around his bat, worry him. With only David Allen, the wicket-keeper, Wes Hall, Charlie and Lance Gibbs left we were in trouble, but I was middling the ball and David seemed to have no problems.

To my surprise, Colin Cowdrey, who had been appointed in place of Mike Smith to take charge of the England team, soon decided to withdraw his attacking field each time I faced the bowling. When the fielders were close, I chose to counter-attack, seeking to drive them away. With so many runs in hand, Cowdrey should have persisted. Instead he set a defensive field and allowed me to take singles so his bowlers could bowl at David. I made no effort to shield David. In my career, I never made an effort to shield any of my partners unless perhaps it was the number eleven.

After tea Cowdrey ordered back his field to David, and I knew we were out of trouble. At the end of the day we had added 193, and the West Indies were 202 ahead. The next day David reached a well-deserved first Test century and was 105 not out when I declared at 369–5, setting England to score 284 in the final four hours. The stand was worth 274, and I was 163 not out. That innings was one of the most satisfying of my life, similar to my 150 on the same ground in 1973. The innings where I had to play in a restrained way were the ones that pleased me – when I had to play in conditions that suited the fielding side.

I was less satisfied with innings on good pitches when the batting side had all the advantages. I made ten centuries against England out of the twenty-six I scored in Test cricket, five in the West Indies and five in England. The two at Lord's were the best, with the 1966 effort the best of all.

Wes and Charlie soon removed Geoff Boycott, Ken Barrington, Cowdrey and Parks in the second innings, but couldn't shift Colin Milburn. Colin kept hooking them into the Mound Stand whenever the ball was dropped short, earning our admiration for his West Indian approach to batting. His unbeaten 126 was a wonderful effort.

The Third Test at Trent Bridge was played on a typical Nottingham pitch of that time – flat and easy-paced – and I knew our first innings of 235 was insufficient. Snow and Higgs, who shared 8 wickets, did the damage, and but for a polished innings of 93 by Seymour Nurse we would have been in much more trouble.

Graveney (109) and Cowdrey (96) were in a stand of 169 in the England innings of 325 before both were magnificently caught, Tom by David Holford in the gully and Cowdrey by Jackie Hendriks. Our openers Hunte and the Barbadian Peter Lashley went for 65 and, as we were still behind, Basil Butcher and Rohan Kanhai started cautiously. They were barracked by the crowd and abused in the press. England had often batted like that, but no one minded. When the West Indies did it, we were assailed!

Once a reasonable lead had been established, Butcher, lucky on several occasions, added 110 with Rohan, enabling me to declare at 482–5. The second half of the innings was conducted at whirlwind speed, Butcher scoring 209, and I came in with a rapid 94.

England's rate was no better than ours had been at the low point of our innings, and we bowled them out for 253, winning by 139 runs and answering our critics.

We clinched the Wisden Trophy at Headingley in August in a match which was one of my most successful Tests in England. I made 174 in our 500, scoring a hundred between lunch and tea in a tand of 265 with Seymour Nurse (137). That was after yet another failure by the openers. That 1966 side was a great team, but how much better it would have been if Conrad Hunte had had a settled partner! We tried Easton McMorris, Joey Carew and Peter Lashley, and none made the position his own.

This time Graveney and Cowdrey failed, and we won by an innings and 55 runs with Gibbs taking 6–39 in the second innings. I managed 8–80 in both innings, bowling a mixture of pace and spin. The only England batsman to stand up against our bowling was Basil d'Oliveira, who hit Wes for a straight six, one of many attractive strokes he played. Basil never liked being pinned down. I first played against him in League cricket, and he used to hit everything out of the ground!

The final Test at the Oval was an anti-climax for us, with Brian Close leading a revamped England side to victory by an innings and 34 runs. The only notable feature from our point of view was that Rohan Kanhai's 104 was his first century in England in 15 Tests. We were dismissed for 268, not enough on a good batting pitch.

England were 166–7 when Graveney and John Murray, recalled in place of Parks, did a Sobers–Holford style recovery act and added 217. Murray, whom I eventually trapped lbw, scored 112. He was a very fine cricketer, a good wicket-keeper and a technically correct batsman. The last pair, Higgs and Snow, then proceeded to add another 128 to take England's total up to 527. That was not a glorious moment for West Indies cricket. And nor was our second innings, all out 225.

Some of our players were nearing the end of their career. I knew they still had some good cricket left in them, but it was time to look for younger replacements in key positions.

14 | The Best Ever West Indies Side

When Clive Lloyd's West Indian side beat England 5–0 in England in 1984 it was said that his team was the best ever to come out of the Caribbean. Clive's team had a phenomenal record – I would not dispute that – and when the West Indies captained by Viv Richards, Clive's successor, beat England 5–0 in the Caribbean in 1985–6 the cry that these players were the best ever was even stronger.

I could not agree with it. The outstanding West Indies team in my opinion was the one I captained between 1965 and 1967. It had a better-balanced attack than Clive's side, better batsmen and a better wicket-keeper. Also the opposition we played in those days was far superior. In 1963, England could call upon John Edrich, Ted Dexter, Ken Barrington, Colin Cowdrey, Brian Close and Jim Parks. I would class that batting line-up well ahead of the one under David Gower's leadership. I would go further: there wasn't one batsman in Gower's side I would put into the 1963 side, not even Gower himself.

Gower's side had no fast bowler to compare with Fred Trueman or Brian Statham. No spin bowler to equal Tony Lock, Fred Titmus or David Allen.

Only in opening batting did Clive Lloyd's team have an advantage over the 1963 and 1966 West Indies touring sides. The Gordon Greenidge–Desmond Haynes partnership was superior, but only because we had no settled partner for Conrad Hunte.

I would rate Conrad above both Gordon and Desmond. He was the outstanding opener of my time in Test cricket from the West

Indies, probably the best of all. He could score quickly, was good all round the wicket and was a brilliant hooker. He was also a very nice man, with a good sense of humour.

As his career developed, he became interested in the Moral Rearmament Movement and naturally found himself ribbed by some of the other players. After that, I found it was less easy to communicate with him. He used to leave notes for people. I remember one note in which he apologised for making a comment about something I had said. I did not think it was worth apologising for, but that was Conrad's way.

Rohan Kanhai was the number three batsman in the 1963 side, and you would have to assess him against Viv Richards, who often used to occupy that position in the West Indies side of the eighties. Viv may have a bigger reputation now in the game than Rohan had, but some of that may be due to the lack of competition. There are fewer players of class around today, so Viv stands out.

In Rohan's day he had to compete with the 'three Ws' – Everton Weekes, Frank Worrell and Clyde Walcott – Seymour Nurse, Conrad Hunte, Basil Butcher, Lawrence Rowe and myself. Rohan's overall Test record is little different from Viv's, and I am sure he faced better bowling. They are so close together I would declare a draw in that contest.

Number four would pitch Seymour Nurse against Larry Gomes, the Trinidadian left-hander. There is no comparison between them. Larry had a reasonable Test record, but Seymour, in my view, was one of the best ever West Indian batsmen. Seymour was twenty-seven when he started his Test career and should have gone on much longer than he did: he retired at thirty-five.

We were in Australia in 1968–9 when he made the decision after a run of low scores. I tried to talk him out of it, especially as we were about to set off on a tour of New Zealand which would give him a chance to redeem himself. 'No, I've written to the selectors to tell them I'm retiring,' he said. 'You know these people. I don't want them to chase me away. I'll make the decision myself.'

I failed to stop him posting the letter, which was a tragedy for him because he was our leading batsman in New Zealand. He made his highest score of 258 there, which was some achievement on New Zealand pitches which tend to favour the bowlers more than in the West Indies or Australia. Seymour still plays for the over-forties in Barbados at the age of fifty-three, and I reckon he is good enough to play for Barbados, so sound is his technique. A Jamaican, Maurice Foster, took his place in the team and he wasn't really in the same class. Maurice used to bowl off-spinners that never turned!

Number five in the order would have to be contested by myself and Clive Lloyd, although we did not appear in that position on too many occasions. I would prefer not to make a decision on that one!

Number six would put Basil Butcher up against an all-rounder in the eighties team, probably Eldine Baptiste. Basil was an underrated batsman who averaged 43 in Tests. Eldine has never been outstanding with either bat or ball.

The contest between the wicket-keepers at number seven is again won by the sixties candidate, Jackie Hendriks. Jackie was in my view the number one West Indies wicket-keeper. He was just as good up to the stumps against the slow bowlers as he was standing back for the quick bowlers. He was very enthusiastic and wouldn't merely remove the bails, but knock all three stumps out of the ground. Jeffrey Dujon was a better batsman, I will concede that, but Jackie made some runs, too. Jackie must win my vote because of his superior wicket-keeping.

Number eight brings together the off-spin bowlers, Lance Gibbs from my day and the current holder of the place, Roger Harper. I have no hesitation in saying Lance was the finest off-spin bowler produced by the West Indies. He learned his trade in Guyana where the pitches are so good for batting that you have to be a master bowler to avoid being hit. Lance was the best hard-wicket spinner of them all. He took his wickets on the flattest of pitches by his control, flight and change of pace. He is still the only West Indies bowler to pass 300 Test wickets. Roger Harper, too, learned his cricket in Guyana and still has a long way to go to reach the standard of Lance. Roger is a superlative fielder and a batsman capable of big scores but, judged as a bowler you want to win

West Indies touring team, 1963 – the best team I ever played in. Back row, left to rig
George Duckworth (scorer), Basil Butcher, Joey Carew, Lester King, Anthony White,
Charlie Griffith, Lance Gibbs, Seymour Nurse, Easton McMorris, Mr D. Pye (masseu
front row, left to right: *Berkeley Gaskin (manager), Willie Rodriguez, Rohan Kanhai,
Alf Valentine, Frank Worrell (captain), Conrad Hunte (vice-captain), myself, Wes Ha
Harold Burnett (assistant manager);* sitting on the grass, left to right: *Deryck Murray
David Allan, Joe Solomon.*

West Indies touring team to England, 1973. Back row, left to right: *Mr L. Pink, Alv
Kallicharran, Inshan Ali, Bernard Julien, Keith Boyce, Vanburn Holder, Grayson
Shillingford, Ron Headley, Maurice Foster, Elquemedo Willett, David Murray;* front
row, left to right: *Esmond Kentish (manager), Deryck Murray, Clive Lloyd, myself,
Rohan Kanhai (captain), Lance Gibbs, Roy Fredericks, Mr G. Gibbs.*

Clive Lloyd square-cutting at Lord's while playing for the Rest of the World in 1970.

The wicketkeeper I have always rated one of the world's best, and the best West Indian of my time – Jackie Hendriks.

Rohan Kanhai plays his famous hook shot in a match against the MCC at Lord's. On many occasions he would end up lying on the pitch!

Some of the great players I have played with or against:

Lance Gibbs

Charlie Griffith

Tony Greig

nny Gavaskar

Richie Benaud

Wes Hall

The nearest I have seen to a tragedy on the cricket field was when Indian Test batsman Nari Contractor ducked into a delivery from Charlie Griffith at Bridgetown in 196. The sound was like eggshells cracking and Nari was rushed to hospital where he underwent emergency surgery. Later he needed another major operation and had a plate inserted in his head. Several players from both sides donated blood.

Australian captain Bobby Simpson signals for help after Jackie Hendriks, the West Indies wicketkeeper, is hit in the head by Graham McKenzie, the Australian fast bo in a Test match in the West Indies. I was batting with Jackie at the time, and also picture are Bill Lawry (to my left) and wicketkeeper Wally Grout.

Knighted by Her Majesty the Queen at the Garrison Racecourse, Barbados, in February 1975.

Two great batsmen in Adelaide in 1981: Sir Donald Bradman, always a great friend and adviser, and current West Indies captain Viv Richards.

e Rest of the World team, which I captained in 1970. Back row, left to right: sharat Hassan (reserve), Intikhab Alam, Mike Procter, Graeme Pollock, Clive Lloyd, aham McKenzie, Barry Richards, Faroukh Engineer; front row, left to right: Rohan nhai, Eddie Barlow, myself, Lance Gibbs.

One of my typical golf shots, which is not too dissimilar to the shot I am playing for the Rest of the World against England's Ray Illingworth at Lord's in 1970!

My other great relaxation is horse-racing, and together with Wes Hall (right) I own a horse called Cruise Missile that has done pretty well in Barbados.

matches, Lance must gain preference. Lance was a wonderful fielder, too. The best gully fielder I ever saw.

The number nine position has to put a spin bowler from the 1963 side, David Holford, against a fast bowler of the present, Malcolm Marshall. I do not doubt Marshall's talent. He has no peer among fast bowlers of the modern generation. But to provide balance in a side I would pick David, a fine leg-break bowler and sound batsman.

If a team wants to win matches anywhere in the world, it has to be able to exploit the conditions. The long winning run of Clive Lloyd's team ended in Sydney when it fell to the leg-spin of Bob Holland.

The pitch took so much turn that Holland proved a match-winner. I would always have a leg-break bowler, or a slow left-hander, in my side in preference to another fast bowler, providing my fast bowlers were great bowlers.

That match in Sydney was one of the few occasions when Clive Lloyd could be accused of making a mistake. Australia went into the game with two spin bowlers – Holland and Murray Bennett – because they thought the pitch would suit spin. Lloyd and his selectors picked a team that did not contain a spin bowler.

The confidence of the Australians had been lifted by Lloyd's decision to bat on in the final day in Melbourne in the Fourth Test when he could have declared. His decision may well have cost his team a twelfth successive Test victory, because with half an hour less to bat the Australians held out to 198–8.

Number ten is between two Barbadians, Charlie Griffith and Joel Garner, both great bowlers in their different styles. Joel took more wickets at a lower cost, but I still maintain Charlie was the more damaging bowler.

Number eleven is another difficult selection: Wes Hall against Michael Holding. Michael's record was marginally better in Test cricket, but as with Joel he was playing against weaker opponents. There was little to choose between them in pace. Michael had the more graceful action and was the better stylist, but Wes was more aggressive.

I believe the 1963 side was stronger because it was better equipped for all conditions. If another fast bowler was required, I could bowl fast. I could bowl at Joel's pace but rarely sustained it because I was needed for other rôles. I used to rely on swing and getting batsmen out by using my brain. And I could also bowl Chinamen and googlies if conditions helped slow bowlers and we needed even more variation.

If the two sides could have met, I am confident my side would have come out on top!

15 | Riot in Calcutta

The most terrifying experience I have had on a cricket-field happened in Calcutta on New Year's Day, 1967. The ground was much smaller than the 100,000 capacity of the present day, catering for about 30,000 people, and that number was swelled to around 40,000 as thousands of extra spectators turned up without tickets for an all-ticket match. The authorities had sold more tickets than they had places, and the surplus fans tried to find places around the boundary ropes.

The West Indies batted first on a pitch which none of the players thought would last the distance; and both openers, Conrad Hunte and Robin Bynoe of Barbados, were run out. I had wanted Bynoe to tour England the previous summer, but the selectors overruled me. He was a very talented player who might have made a successful partner for Hunte if he had been given a reasonable chance.

I was number seven in a very strong batting line-up and still to go in when the crowd, encroaching further and further on to the playing-arena, erupted into a full-scale riot. The police tried to push them back, unavailingly, and finally resorted to a charge, which was like putting a lighted match to a firework.

We were told that a spectator had been hit in the eye by a policeman's baton and that inflamed the crowd. The players quickly returned to the dressing-room, fearful of what might happen to them.

The police tried tear-gas. That failed. And so did their charge. They then proceeded to leave the scene in disorder, leaving the incensed spectators covering the whole of the pitch. The average

Indian is a very placid, serene individual, but if he is roused he can be violent.

The scenes that followed were unprecedented at a Test match. People started tearing down stands and setting fire to them. Chairs and other furniture were hurled into the flames. There were not merely a few hundred people involved. It seemed as if thousands of them were tearing the place apart.

The tear-gas swept into the dressing room, and the players were coughing and choking. The order went out: 'Stay where you are. Do not leave.' Conrad Hunte was concerned about the West Indies flag, which was still flying above the pavilion.

'Come with me and I'll get it back,' he said to me.

'Go out there?' I said. 'You must be crazy.'

I believe Conrad did rescue the flag – and singlehandedly, too!

There was a door at the rear of the dressing-room, and Charlie Griffith opened it. Behind was a galvanised tin sheet. Charlie sent it crashing, and we stepped through the gap on to the road outside. People were milling around in confusion. An Indian was at the wheel of a small car. Not wanting to stay in the vicinity a moment longer, six of us accepted his offer of a ride.

Charlie declined the invitation. He may have been suspicious of where we were being taken! So he set off to run the two miles to the team hotel. We passed him a few hundred yards further down the crowded street.

There was destruction and disorder all around us. Buses were hijacked then set on fire, and every time we passed a sports-ground flames appeared from the wooden pavilions. When the team finally assembled at the hotel, the management discussed what should be done. The players were in favour of abandoning the match and the tour returning home.

A local official said: 'That would not be wise. We cannot guarantee what will happen. If the people know where you are going, the bus might be stopped on the way to the airport and set on fire with you inside.'

We decided to stay on! The next day's play was cancelled while clearing-up went on, and we stayed at our hotel. The next day was a scheduled rest-day, so three days had elapsed when we returned to the ground for the resumption of play.

We were amazed to find that there was no sign of any disturbance. It was as though nothing had occurred, that it was all a bad dream. The game began on time, I scored 70 in eighty minutes and we went on to win by an innings and 45 runs. Although I did not score a century in the series, I averaged 114. The Indians were an improving side, and I had to play a number of painstaking innings to get us out of trouble.

I enjoyed touring India. It was my favourite country to visit, but I did not want to make that tour because I was tired after leading the West Indies to victory in England in 1966. I had been playing cricket all year and needed a break. After returning from the trip to England, I told the selectors that they should groom a younger player in my place and save me for the visit of England to the Caribbean at the end of the year.

The selectors would not accept my arguments. Jeffrey Stollmeyer said: 'You are public property. The Indians want you, and you have to go.' I was very angry. I had played for the West Indies for twelve years without respite and also played in the domestic cricket in England and in Australia. I needed time off to rekindle my enthusiasm.

I pleaded with the selectors, Frank Worrell among them. He thought I should go. It was not a question of money. I was not offered any more, and it would not have made any difference anyway. Eventually, I conceded that I should make myself available. I was glad that I went, for it was one of my most successful tours abroad.

After winning the first two Tests, superb bowling by Erapalli Prasanna and Bishen Bedi nearly brought the Indians success in Madras, but Charlie Griffith and I thwarted them with an eighth-wicket stand of 77 in the final ninety minutes.

Charlie, delighted to be promoted above his great rival Wes Hall, upset the Indians by sticking his left leg English-style right down the pitch and denying the Indian spinners. He got so far down that sometimes the ball hit him on the chest. The leg-spin bowler

Chandrasekhar was quite pacey, and some of the blows were painful. Charlie didn't flinch.

Chandra didn't like some of the bouncers Charlie bowled in the series and on the final day he sought his revenge! Charlie showed great character. He was a good man to have in your side.

Chandra took 242 Test wickets, including a large number against England, but I never had any trouble with him. He was not a big spinner of the ball and bowled very few leg-breaks. His stock ball was the straight one which tended to bounce because of his high arm action, and the googly.

Led by an excellent captain in the Nawab of Pataudi, known as 'Tiger' to his friends, the Indians were developing into a good enough side to win successive series against England. They had a monopoly of the world's leading spin bowlers.

Bedi, the turbaned Sikh, was one of the best slow left-hand bowlers the game has known. There was little to choose between him and Alf Valentine when Val was in his prime. He had more variety, took more wickets in Tests (226 to Val's 139) and lasted longer at the top level.

Bedi's bowling was full of craft and guile. He flighted the ball and also had the ability to hold it back. Batsmen would stretch for it and find it wasn't quite there, mistiming their shot and often giving a catch. He changed his pace so subtly that the victim rarely knew what was happening.

I loved playing against him. He was a courageous player. If he threw the ball up and you drove it for six, he would throw the next one up. He never ducked a challenge. He liked players to go for his bowling. 'It gives me more chance to get them out,' he said. That should be the philosophy of the spin bowler. If he pushes the ball through because he is frightened of being hit, the batsman will hold back. The game will become a stalemate. That was never my way of playing cricket. Like Bedi, I wanted adventure and fun. I wanted to attack all the time.

The Indians had another left-arm spinner in that era, Salim Durani, and though not in the class of Bedi he was a much underrated bowler. For some reason, the selectors did not seem to like him. Later on, he became a successful movie actor.

Just as the West Indies have produced a string of fast bowlers in the past few years, so the Indians kept up a steady supply of quality spin bowlers. Another slow left-armer, Bapu Nadkarni, was one of the meanest bowlers I have played against. He once bowled a record number of maiden overs in a Test match and would race out on either side of the wicket to prevent singles. He was one of the few bowlers I saw run to point to eliminate the chance of a quick single!

The leading Indian off-spinner in my time, though the Indian selectors did not agree too often with that view, was Prasanna. He flighted the ball more than the man who kept him out on occasions, Venkataraghavan. On many occasions they played together in the same side.

The Indians also had a number of world-class leg-spin and googly bowlers including Chandra Borde and Subash Gupte. Borde was accurate and bowled with a high looping action. He was also a Test-class batsman. In my opinion, Gupte was the best leg-spinner of my time in cricket – better than Richie Benaud or, from the modern day, Abdul Qadir.

I have not played against Qadir, but from watching him I have decided he does not think enough about his game. I saw him bowl round the wicket to a left-hander in Australia, which was not a very intelligent thing to do. I spoke to Intikhab, one of his predecessors in the Pakistan side, an accurate leg-spinner himself who maybe could have turned the ball a shade more, and Inti said Qadir was not a man who responded to well-intentioned advice. I believe all crick-eters, however good, can benefit from advice from those with experience, players who have proved themselves.

Nevertheless, Qadir is a good bowler, as he has proved with more than 180 Test wickets. He is a big spinner of the ball and has good control and disguise of his googly.

West Indies crowds love cricket and appreciate its finer points. But there have been a number of occasions when their enthusiasm has spilled over into violence. The 1953–4 tour by Sir Len Hutton's team was marred by several incidents, provoked chiefly by controversial umpiring decisions. All the problems had been resolved by the time I made my Test début in the Fifth Test in Kingston.

West Indies supporters are noisy and boisterous, and if they think one of their players has suffered an injustice they can become very angry. I had some experience of how a minor incident can escalate into crowd trouble during the Second Test against England in Kingston on the 1967–8 tour when Basil Butcher was given out caught down the leg side by Jim Parks off the bowling of Basil d'Oliveira.

The West Indies were striving to avoid defeat on one of the worst pitches ever prepared at Sabina Park, and the crowd didn't like the decision. It looked a legitimate one to those of us near the bat, but bottles started to rain down as David Holford came in to replace Butcher.

I was batting at the time and, together with the England captain Colin Cowdrey, went over towards the section of the crowd where the bottles were being thrown in an attempt to restore order. It soon became obvious that there was nothing we could do. Colin was keen to continue his peacemaking rôle.

'They're not going to take any notice,' I said. 'They're so mad no one is going to pacify them.'

I turned away, leaving Colin still trying to remonstrate with them. Police officers arrived with tear-gas, which they started to fire only to see the gas blow back towards the pavilion. The players and officials were off the field by this time.

A few extremists start the trouble and are followed by others. A combination of things causes it – drink, betting and frustration. But, once an hour or so goes by, my experience is that it soon calms down. The genuine supporters soon recognise that they are missing their cricket.

The pitch for that match was the oddest I ever saw in Kingston. When we inspected it before the start, it had wide cracks, and Tom Graveney said to Lance Gibbs: 'Hey, Lance, you better not walk across it.' Lance, tall and very slim, looked at him quizzically. 'We wouldn't want you to fall through one of those cracks!' said Tom.

England somehow managed to score 376, with John Edrich (96) and Cowdrey (101) showing immense concentration and determination. Steve Camacho, now secretary of the West Indies Board of Control, was bowled by a shooter. In Trinidad the shooter is known as a 'rat' or a 'snake', and there were plenty to follow that day in Kingston. I had one myself – first ball. John Snow was the bowler, and before I could get my bat down the ball skidded through, hit me on the boot and I was out.

The West Indies were out for 143, with Snow, one of England's most successful pace bowlers of the postwar years, taking 7–49. There was little doubt that Cowdrey would enforce the follow-on. I have always claimed to be an optimist and, even at 230 behind on a substandard pitch, I still felt we could survive. Cricket matches, like battles, are often turned by hunches that came off.

I claim no credit for the one that enabled us to escape in that Test match. At the end of our innings Seymour Nurse, who was at 4 in the first innings, came to me and asked if he could open. We had used Deryck Murray in the first innings, and Deryck was out for 0. Deryck played a number of fine innings for us over the years but was no opener. And I did not want to risk our wicket-keeper against the new ball on such a dangerous pitch. A blow on the finger could put him out of the match.

I readily agreed to Seymour's suggestion. He batted beautifully for his 73 and, though deliveries were still squatting or lifting throat-high, I realised the fortunes of the game were changing rapidly. We now had a chance of avoiding what seemed to be an inevitable defeat. Camacho and Clive Lloyd fell to 'snakes', and when I came in at 174–4 we still faced the prospect of defeat. I was on a 'pair', two noughts in the same game.

David Brown, the England fast bowler from Warwickshire, was the bowler and, expecting another shooter, I went forward to the first ball. Instead of keeping low, it bounced sharply off a length and, as I tried to adjust, the ball came off the bat-handle and looped over the head of Fred Titmus at short leg. Fred was the smallest man in the England side. If he had been a bigger man, I might have gone. That was the closest I came to getting a 'pair'.

After d'Oliveira dropped me at slip when 7, I knew that it was my day. The later batsmen – Butcher at seven (that revealed the strength of our batting line-up in those days), Holford at eight and Griffith at nine – helped me hoist the total to an unexpected 391 before I declared with 9 wickets down, setting England 159 in eighty-five minutes plus the extra seventy-five minutes they asked to be played on the sixth day to compensate for the amount of play lost in the riot.

I was forced to be so cautious that I went from 88 to my century with twelve successive singles. My beaten 113 had to rate as one of my most responsible innings. England lost 4 wickets for 19 runs before bad light ended play, with me bowling Geoff Boycott with the inswinger for 0.

I don't think Geoff relished that delivery. I dismissed him with it on a number of occasions. After one such dismissal, I met him afterwards and chided him. 'You've got a technical weakness,' I said. 'You put your front pad too far across, and it stops you getting your bat into line. You should put your pad more down the pitch, not across.'

Geoff was always keen to discuss technique, especially his own, and was grateful for the advice. In a subsequent match he followed my advice and was caught! He wasn't too happy when I met him later. 'What I told you was for the inner,' I said. 'But you've got to work out yourself what to do about the outer, the one that goes the other way!'

Next morning England must have regretted asking for those extra seventy-five minutes. Four more wickets went down, and there was a lot of playing and missing, appealing and high tension. Jim Parks, whom I rated a good player on hard pitches, was unlucky enough to be struck by one of the nastiest deliveries of the match: a ball from Wes Hall which reared up and hit him in the Adam's apple. Fortunately, it did no serious damage. England finished holding on at 68–8.

David Brown and John Snow were contrasting bowlers. I liked David as a man and as a cricketer. Off the field we had much in common. We were both interested in horses, and his wife was a jockey. On it, he was a wholehearted bowler who would try to bowl just as quickly if conditions were against him as he would when they favoured him.

Snow was the better all-round performer but was very temperamental. If he felt he was getting no help, he would want to come off. He chided batsmen if they played or missed or nicked the ball through the slips. He said a few things to me over the years, but I never took much notice.

I came up against 'sledging' as it is called in Australia on a few occasions. I would never indulge in it myself, or condone it. Nor would I allow it to affect my concentration.

16 | The Last of the Walkers?

I always 'walked' if I thought I was out caught when batting. At the start of my professional career there were a number of players who made the umpire's decision for him and 'walked'.

Nowadays, I doubt if there is a single top-class player who 'walks'. The rewards are so great for success that anyone who did so would incur the wrath of his colleagues. Yet when a batsman stays at the crease after he knows he is out and the umpire has reprieved him he is often greeted with accusations of cheating from the fielders.

Those same fielders wouldn't 'walk', so it seems strange that they should be so righteous. It is human nature, though: they want the batsman out and are aggrieved when he stays.

There was not a single instance in my career when I failed to 'walk' when I knew I had snicked the ball. If I got a touch early on and stayed, eventually reaching a big score, I would have been disgusted with myself. The batsman knows if he has touched the ball. Sometimes the nick can be so imperceptible, the ball barely brushing the bat, that only the batsman is aware of what has happened.

There was even one occasion in Australia when I walked without an appeal being made. I knew I had touched the ball, and it was only when I started to go towards the pavilion that the late Wally Grout, the Australian wicket-keeper, shouted: 'Howzat?' The umpire raised his finger, and Wally said: 'I didn't know you snicked that. Thanks very much!'

Some batsmen defend themselves against the charge of sharp practice by saying why 'walk' if you do not have the right to tell an umpire you have hit the ball when he has given you out lbw. I do not accept that. If the umpire has made an honest mistake, the batsman can only accept it. On another occasion his mistake may favour the batsman.

Frank Worrell, the man I idolised more than any other cricketer, always 'walked', and Conrad Hunte used to later in his career after he joined the Moral Rearmament movement. Conrad tended to be selective about 'walking' early in his career. Some players 'walk' after they have passed 100, when it no longer matters. I do not think that is in the right spirit of the game. You either have a principle or you don't.

The former England captain Colin Cowdrey 'walked', but not always. The only Australian I knew who did was the batsman Brian Booth, who played 29 Tests in the early sixties. I never discovered a walker in either India or Pakistan. In those countries, there is sometimes a reluctance to give certain players out as though the umpires are unwilling to deny the spectators and themselves the chance of seeing a classic innings.

The only time I stayed at the crease and waited for the umpire's decision was if there was some doubt about a catch carrying to the fielder. If the fielder said he had made a clean catch and I thought there was no reason to doubt his word, I would 'walk'.

One of the few times I had been really annoyed on the cricket-field was when Basil d'Oliveira refused to go in the Fourth Test at Headingley in 1966 when Conrad Hunte claimed he had made a clean diving catch off a drive to mid-wicket. England were 179–7, and Dolly was in the sixties. Conrad threw himself at the ball and scooped it up. It appeared to be a good catch to me, and Conrad confirmed it by shouting: 'I caught it, I caught it.'

To our amazement, Dolly remained unmoved, and the umpire Charlie Elliott made no attempt to enquire further into the matter. Realising that Dolly wasn't going to be sporting about it, the whole West Indies side appealed en masse. Charlie Elliott shook his head.

I was furious. 'You are a blasted cheat,' I said to Dolly. 'You know Conrad don't tell lies.'

Dolly was unaffected. 'I didn't think it carried,' he said. 'And the umpire didn't give me out.'

I didn't let it rest. When Lance Gibbs was bowling and I was crouching a few feet in the rear of Dolly at leg slip I would mutter: 'You're a cheat!' When Charlie Griffith had him caught by Wes Hall at 88 none of us applauded him. I am told that Conrad might have done, which wasn't surprising. After we had won, several of the English players, including Tom Graveney, Colin Cowdrey and Dolly, came in for a drink.

I have always believed that any disputes on the field of play should be forgotten when play finishes, and that was the case this time. I offered Dolly a drink. Neither of us had any hard feelings.

I played against Dolly on many occasions in League cricket when he was with Middleton and I played for Radcliffe. He was an underrated player. In those days he hit the ball with great power, usually with a cross-bat. He was a difficult man to bowl to because he would always be looking to hit the ball to the boundary.

After joining Worcestershire, he became a more refined player and learned more about defending. He could still hit the ball very hard! As a bowler, he was also a great asset to his side. His control was good and his most dangerous delivery was the one that went straight on!

That was because he usually bowled off-cutters and he could bowl the straight one with the same cutting action. The batsman expected the ball to come back to him from the off, and when it didn't he was in trouble. Dolly could also bowl off-breaks and was a useful fielder. He was an all-rounder in the true sense and a valuable acquisition for his adopted country.

Worcestershire had a reasonable side in those days. Vanburn Holder, who played under me on numerous occasions, wasn't as fast as some of today's West Indian bowlers but was lively and had the art of control. Ron Headley, son of the legendary George Headley, opened for Worcestershire for many years and played two Tests against England in 1973.

I believed he was a good enough player to have played many more Tests than that, especially as the West Indies were always looking for a partner for Conrad Hunte in the sixties. I wanted Ron to be picked for the 1969 tour, but the other five selectors did not agree with my thinking.

In England, the Test and County Cricket Board have been experimenting with electronic aids supposedly to make life easier for umpires. These days umpires are under greater pressure than they have ever been in the past, with almost every decision they make being scrutinised and replayed on television.

Umpires are exposed to countless inquests during Test and one-day matches at international level. I believe this pressure has made it less likely that umpires can survive as long as the John Langridges and Tommy Spencers, who were in their late sixties when they finally retired.

Would their jobs be any easier if they had access to electronic aids? I do not think so. I think the game would be reduced to a farce. Imagine what would happen. A batsman is hit on the pads and play is held up while the umpires seek the advice of a third umpire off the field who is studying a television monitor. The view of the third umpire is relayed to the umpire in the middle by walkie-talkie. The umpires then reconsider on the basis of the new information. Finally, they make their decision. If the over rate in Tests is down to twelve an hour, which is the case sometimes, it will drop to eight an hour if this has to happen every time there is an lbw appeal!

The TCCB's idea, apparently, was that two television cameras should be trained on the batsman and if the ball hit the pad between line and line of the wicket and would have struck the wicket a signal would be conveyed to the umpire advising an 'out'. But the company experimenting with the idea advised the Board that it would need a large sum of money to continue the experiments, and the Board wisely abandoned the project.

The other idea which the Board investigated was to install a device in the handle of the bat which would send a signal to a device lodged with the umpire if contact was made with the ball. This would allow the umpire to be certain that the batsman had hit the ball when there was an appeal for a catch.

Which batsman would allow the authorities to fit such a device to his bat? He would claim it was an infringement of his freedom to ply his trade! The Board might face a costly court action!

These matters must be left to the discretion of the man in the best position with the best view: the umpire. Only he can decide if a batsman is out. If he makes a mistake, cricketers will accept that it is an honest mistake. Pakistan objected to one of England's most experienced umpires, David Constant, in the 1987 series in England, but that is exceptional. The touring side nearly always approves the appointment of home umpires. And English umpires are still acknowledged as the best in the world, chiefly because they umpire seven days a week and have more chance to improve.

Whenever there is an umpiring controversy, the idea of appointing neutral umpires is mooted. There were neutral umpires in the last World Cup in India and Pakistan. I do not object to a panel of the world's leading umpires being appointed for a competition of that sort as long as every country hosting it follows this practice.

But I would not like to see neutral umpires in normal Test cricket. Why has the subject arisen? It is because there is a suspicion that umpires from the host country will favour the home team. That may be so on occasion, but might not a neutral umpire – say, an English umpire officiating in India – give Viv Richards the benefit of the doubt because, like the spectators, he wants to see Viv bat?

It is usual to see English umpires like the popular Dickie Bird officiating abroad. How many times, though, do overseas umpires officiate in English county cricket? It has not happened too much. The Pakistanis had neutral umpires during their series against India in 1987, but would other countries – say, England and Australia – accept Pakistani umpires? If they didn't, there would be little work at Test level for Pakistani umpires.

In my opinion three of the outstanding umpires in recent years have been Sid Buller, Charlie Elliott from England and Col Egar from Australia. All of them loved the game, understood it and played it.

When they made a decision, they would explain it to the bowler. 'That was missing leg,' they would say. They did not make hasty decisions. Umpires need to concentrate every second of the game, and the demands on their powers of concentration are far greater than those on batsmen. It is a most demanding occupation. With so many prizes at stake, the pressure has never been greater.

Dickie Bird relieves the tension by continual chat and banter. He never stops. He is never out of the game, and the players respect him because he usually makes the right decision.

One of the few umpires to vex me was the late Fred Price, who no-balled me for overstepping on one tour of England. I was upset because I made a practice of never bowling no balls. I knew how important they were to the batting side. Nothing is more frustrating than to dismiss a batsman only for the umpire to shout 'No ball'. In my twenty years in the game I bowled less than half a dozen no balls.

During the 1957 tour of England by the West Indies, Wes Hall was bowling a dozen or more an innings. We tried many ways to try to cure his problem, without success. He missed a subsequent tour by Pakistan because he was still no-balling. It took him a long time to find a solution.

One of my favourite umpiring characters was the Australian all-rounder Cec Pepper. He ribbed his fellow-Australian cricketers when he umpired their matches, possibly because he was bitter that he had never been selected for his country. 'I'll give those bastards nothing,' he used to say. 'Look at them – can't even play the ——— game.'

He would use a swear word in every sentence, and that may have been one of the reasons why his undoubted talents as a player did not take him further. I used to play against him in League cricket and knew from my own experience just how much ability he possessed. He was a leg-break and googly bowler who had the most deadly 'flipper' I ever encountered.

He squeezed it out of his side like squashing an egg, and it skidded through barely a foot off the ground. Frank Worrell warned me about him. 'If he drops it a bit short, never go across the line,' he said. The first time I played against Cec I was on about 20 when he bowled a delivery just short of a length. I lifted my bat, preparing to pull the ball to leg, when I remembered Frank's advice. Hastily, my bat just managed to jab down on the ball.

'That ———— Worrell has been talking to you,' he said.

The stories about him filled many hours of happy reminiscing over a drink in the League. He bowled at a batsman once, it was said, who was unable to get a bat to a single delivery. Cec was supposed to have said: 'You can open your eyes now. The over's finished.'

In one match the batting side needed a boundary to win and they achieved the target when a fielder let the ball through his legs on the boundary. Cec was the unfortunate bowler, and as the players trooped off a colleague said: 'If he'd kept his legs together, he'd have stopped that.'

'That wasn't the problem,' said Cec. 'His ———— mother should have kept her legs together a long time ago.'

The only time I felt resentful about umpires was in 1958–9 when the West Indies went to India and Pakistan, won the series in India and lost 2–1 in Pakistan. There were few problems on the field in India. I made three centuries, averaged 92.83 and took a few wickets. I found India a fascinating country. There was no opportunity to have a night out in the West Indian sense, because it was not possible to buy alcohol. We were issued with permits once a month, which we pooled to buy whisky. But there were not many tots per man. The people were courteous and helpful, the pitches good and the crowds enthusiastic.

My mood changed on arrival in Karachi after a comment by one of the leading cricket officials who had seen me score more than 1000 runs in the series in India. 'This Garry Sobers will not make a single hundred here,' he said.

One of the officials of our team said: 'Don't bet on that. Sobers is likely to make a hundred any place.'

The man was adamant. 'I tell you, not in Pakistan he won't.'

I was not present at the time but I was told of the conversation later. It disturbed me greatly.

The First Test took place on the matting pitch in Karachi, and when I arrived at the crease at 62–2 Fazal Mahmood, Pakistan's captain, was bowling. Fazal was one of the best medium-pace bowlers I encountered in my career and on the mat he was a difficult bowler to master.

Before I scored, Fazal struck me on the right pad as I played and missed, everyone appealed and I was given out. I liked to think I knew where my foot was in relation to the stumps and I was certain that the ball would not have hit the wicket. It was going so wide it probably would not have hit another set of stumps. I never argued with umpires, so I departed.

In the dressing-room, some of the other players consoled me. 'I can't understand it,' I said. 'That ball was missing my leg stump by a yard.'

In the second innings, Fazal was again bowling when I came in. I played the ball on to my pads. The ball bounced away, and Aijaz Butt, thinking that there was a chance to catch me, dived and missed it.

I should have been relieved. But Fazal appealed, and up went the umpire's finger. 'What was that for ?' asked Aijaz. 'I dunno,' I said. For the second time in the match I was out lbw in the scorebook but not in reality.

Collie Smith, batting at the other end, made an angry comment to Fazal about what he thought of the appeal and the decision. I felt like joining in, but said nothing as I marched off.

In the dressing-room I let my feelings come out. I started packing my bag. 'I've had enough of this,' I said. 'I'm off home.' Berkeley Gaskin, the manager, asked me not to be hasty.

It was a long, long time before I cooled down and accepted that there would be serious repercussions on my career if I quit. That second dismissal in Karachi gave Fazal his hundredth Test wicket, and I was again one of his lbw victims in the Second Test at Dacca. He captured 12 wickets for 100 runs as Pakistan won by 10 wickets.

In my whole Test career of 160 innings, I was only lbw on sixteen occasions, three of them in the space of sixteen days to Fazal in Pakistan! In that Dacca Test our skipper, Gerry Alexander, was given out stumped when he said his foot was over the crease. He was very angry when he returned to the dressing-room. 'Now you know what it is like to be cheated of your wicket!' I said.

The third and final Test was played on grass in Lahore, and we were happier – particularly Wes Hall, who took a hat trick. Only one of his hat-trick victims needed the intervention of the umpire: Mushtaq Mohammad, who was lbw. That was the match when Mushtaq made his début at the age of 15 years 124 days to become the youngest player ever to play in a Test.

Before the series began in Pakistan, the West Indies objected to one of the umpires on the list submitted to them by the home Board. His name was Idris Beg. We had not seen him in action but had heard enough from other people to know that he might be suspect. A few years earlier, some of the touring English team were so upset at his decisions that they played a practical joke on him which went wrong. They lured him into a room, sat him on a chair and upset a pail of water, suspended from the roof, all over him. They called it 'the water treatment', but the authorities at Lord's did not see it as a joke and the players were reprimanded.

Normally West Indies cricketers have a sporting reputation and they are known to accept the verdict of the umpire without question. An exception was on the second day of the Test match at Edgbaston in 1973 when fielders thought Geoff Boycott was caught by wicket-keeper Deryck Murray off the bowling of Keith Boyce. Umpire Arthur Fagg said not out, and Rohan Kanhai, out to make a success of his first tour abroad as skipper, was most unhappy at the decision.

He was keyed up, as one would expect, but he went too far in showing his displeasure. And he didn't let the matter drop. He kept on about it for the rest of the session. It shouldn't have happened: he was captain, and it was his responsibility to see that decisions were accepted in the right spirit.

Boycott had been the main obstacle to us in the First Test, scoring 97 and 30, and his was the prized wicket in the England side at the time. To be denied his wicket when it looked out was disappointing, but Rohan should have let it go.

It was not the first time a batsman appeared out only for the umpire to disagree. These things happen on the cricket-field. Arthur Fagg was a very experienced and conscientious umpire who had played a lot of cricket at the highest level. He knew the game and was respected. He looked aggrieved, but I cannot recall him saying anything on the field that evening which suggested he was about to walk out.

Something may have been said to our manager, Esmond Kentish, because the next morning Alan Oakman, the former Sussex and England all-rounder and former umpire, came out with Dickie Bird. There was no sign of Fagg. Three of the daily newspapers quoted him as saying he was so disturbed by Kanhai's behaviour that he was quitting the match. He felt that the West Indies no longer had any respect for him.

That was not the case, and Mr Kentish issued a statement saying: 'We are fully satisfied with Arthur Fagg's umpiring.' I think an apology might have been offered as well, for after one over Mr Fagg resumed his position and Alan Oakman retired.

17 | Lost Ball in Swansea

I became the first cricketer to hit six sixes in an over in first-class cricket when I took 36 off an over from Malcolm Nash in Swansea on 31 August 1968. Malcolm, who was twenty-three at the time, showed no sign of being upset. As we strolled to the BBC box to be interviewed afterwards, I said to him: 'You seem perky for a man who has just been hit for a cricket record.'

'And why not?' he replied. 'You're not the only one who goes into the record-books, you know. I do, too!' He is now known as the man who was hit for six sixes but he was a very useful county cricketer.

According to the records, the previous record was 34 by the English batsman Edwin Alletson, who played for Nottinghamshire between 1908 and 1914, at Hove in 1911. But there were two no balls in that over, and he failed to score off one delivery. Alletson went on to make 189 in ninety minutes, and I am told he did little afterwards in his career and faded out. My record was eventually equalled by the Indian all-rounder Ravi Shastri in Bombay in 1984–5. He struck six sixes in an over off a bowler named Tilak Raj and went on to score 200 in 113 minutes.

Malcolm Nash was to be involved in a near-miss in 1977 when Frank Hayes, the Lancashire batsman, took 34 off one of his overs, also at the St Helen's Ground in Swansea. Frank had no chance of emulating my feat because the second ball went for four.

I had no thoughts of breaking a record when I went to the crease in Swansea. Both Glamorgan and Nottinghamshire were high in the table, and we needed a win to clinch a bet I had made with Bunty Ames the previous April in the West Indies when Les Ames, the former Kent and England wicket-keeper, was manager of the MCC side as it was then known (later to be given its proper name, England).

Bunty and I were talking, and she suddenly said: 'I see you will be playing for Nottinghamshire in the county championship this year.' It was a surprise to me, because I had not heard from my agent, the late Bagenal Harvey. Several counties bid for my services after the Test and County Cricket Board decided to allow instant registration for overseas players in time for the 1968 season. In previous years I had had two approaches to play county cricket, one from Ken Graveney of Gloucestershire and the other from Ken Turner, of Northamptonshire, secretary-manager of Leicestershire. At the time overseas players had to serve a two-year qualification before they were eligible to play, and I told both men that I was not prepared to waste two years of my career playing in the second eleven waiting to qualify.

The regulation said players would have to take up residence in the county through the year, and that would have meant leaving Test cricket. I was not prepared to do that. One player who had spent time qualifying in England was Roy Marshall at Hampshire, and he was lost to West Indies cricket though he was one of the best attacking batsmen the West Indies have produced.

The lifting of the ban by the TCCB came a little late for me. I would have preferred it to have happened five or six years earlier when I was fitter and in my prime. I still felt I had a lot to offer, but I was thirty-two and had played fourteen years of non-stop cricket around the world.

I was playing for Norton when it was announced that overseas players would be admitted in 1968. Bagenal Harvey, who started his career in sport as business adviser to Denis Compton, represented me in England and sifted through the offers from the counties. Lancashire, whose players and secretary Jack Wood I knew well, also made an offer, and I believe there were four counties involved. Bagenal accepted the offer from Nottinghamshire because it was the best: £5000 a year salary, accommodation, a car and fares home. Trent Bridge suited me. It was one of the best batting pitches

in the country – in the days before they used to leave the grass on! –
and I had previously made two double centuries there for the West
Indies.

The team had been near the bottom in previous seasons and had
no Test players or players on the fringe of the England side. They
were mostly good professionals, no stars but a lot of hard workers
and enthusiasts.

Bunty Ames asked me how I thought I would fare with them.

'I'll get them to the top four,' I said. It was a rash statement to
make, because I hadn't met their players and knew little about their
strengths and weaknesses.

'They're not that good,' she said. 'Do you want to bet on it?'

I was not a man to spurn a bet, and she promised she would give
me six bottles of champagne if I managed to lift Nottinghamshire
into the top six by the end of the season. The eighteen points we
gained from a victory over Glamorgan by 166 runs confirmed us in
fourth place, and Bunty duly handed over the champagne at a John
Player League match in Kent which followed the next Sunday!

The score was 300–5 when I arrived at the crease in the last
session. Brian Bolus had hit a first-class 140, and we were in a strong
position. When I came to Nottinghamshire, I was appointed captain in place of Norman Hill, and I heard that Bolus was unhappy
about it because he thought he should have got the job. He never
said anything to me on the matter and supported me loyally.

There was less than an hour left, and I wanted to score as quickly
as possible because the pitch was wearing, as it usually did at the St
Helen's Ground, and I wanted the Glamorgan side to bat before the
close. I was 40 not out when the over which was to go into the
history-books began. Malcolm had opened the innings bowling
medium-pace, but he had switched to his slower style in the Derek
Underwood mould – left-arm over the wicket.

There was a short boundary on the Gorse Lane side of the
ground, by the scorebox, and I made up my mind to hit the ball over
it irrespective of where it was pitched. My intention was to swing so
hard at each ball that even a mishit would clear the rope. Malcolm's
first four deliveries, all straight, sailed over the boundary into a

crowd which was becoming more and more excited. A Welshman was being punished, but they sensed a record was within my grasp and were cheering me on. Up in the BBC box filming was supposed to end for the day, but the producer ordered the cameraman to keep filming until the end of the over. Luckily he did, because the film of my exploit is now a valued part of the game's history.

With two balls to go, I said to myself: I can do this. Give it a go. The fifth ball was slightly wide of my off stump, and I failed to get hold of it properly. It went high in the air down to long off where Roger Davis caught it, but the impact forced him back over the line. I thought there was little doubt it was a six, but the umpires, John Langridge and Eddie Phillipson, decided to confer.

The crowd chanted 'six, six, six', and eventually John Langridge's arms were raised signalling the six. In England the law about sixes has been changed on a number of occasions and, if I remember rightly, there was an experimental rule which said a batsman could be out in these circumstances if the catch was completed before the player went over the line.

The delay seemed endless. Tony Lewis, the Glamorgan captain, put all his fielders around the boundary, most of them on the leg side, and Malcolm prepared to bowl the sixth ball. I reasoned that he would try to change his pace and maybe bowl a quicker ball. All my previous five shots had been the same. A change of pace might bring about a mishit, and a catch. A modern bowler, with years of experience bowling in one-day matches, might well have drilled a quicker ball in on my toes, one of the most difficult deliveries to hit for six. But Malcolm was trying to get me out. He was an attacking bowler.

The ball dropped short on middle stump, and I connected in the middle of the bat. It soared out over the wall and into a road outside. 'It's gone clean into Swansea,' said an excited Wilf Wooller, who was combining his job as Glamorgan secretary with the rôle of BBC commentator. The ball wasn't recovered that night. On Monday morning a small boy arrived at the ground and handed a cricket ball to Wilf. 'Is this the ball that Mr Sobers hit for six on Saturday?' he said. Wilf asked him where he had found it. 'It was still rolling down the street when I picked it up,' he said. Later, it was mounted and sent to the Trent Bridge museum.

I promptly declared the innings at 394–5 with my total on 76. I had been in about thirty-eight minutes and might well have completed the quickest hundred for many years, but I wasn't interested in personal records, only the success of any team I might be playing for.

In the dressing-room afterwards some of the fielders took the mickey out of Malcolm Nash about his bowling, and Nash responded by saying that he thought he'd write a book about his experiences. What would it be called? someone asked, and another team mate suggested *Gone with the Wind*!

There were lots of characters in that Nottinghamshire side. When I first met them in the dressing-room, the Jamaican pace bowler Carlton Forbes was lying on the massage-table, and as I passed I couldn't help looking at his big feet. The soles of my feet are white, like those of most black men. But Carlton's were black. He is a very black man.

I started laughing. Carlton joined me; he knew what had amused me. I have never met anyone in cricket who laughed as much as Carlton. Even in the most serious situation he would be smiling. 'I'll tell you a story,' he said. 'The first time I came here I was riding a bike when a big black hand stuck up in front of me, and I stopped. It was a policeman, and I don't know how he managed to see me in the first place because I had no lights. "Excuse me, sir," he said. "Do you realise you are riding without lights?" I flashed a smile at him, showing my white teeth, and he said: "That's better, sir. Why didn't you put your light on before?"'

The club had some useful batsmen in Mike 'Pasty' Harris, the Cornishman, and the two Yorkshiremen, Brian Bolus and Mike Smedley. Bolus went on to play for England, and I thought Smedley might have followed him. Another character was Basharat Hassan, known to everyone as 'Basher', who was born in Nairobi. 'Basher' had a peculiar crouching style similar to the Indian Test player Ramchand and was rather unpredictable. He was an outstanding fielder and in his forties was still good enough to field at short leg for England as a stand-in fielder.

'Dusty' Hare, the England rugby international, was on the staff at the time and was a fair cricketer. The most promising of the batsmen was a young man by the name of Derek Randall. When he was twenty-one I thought Derek should have been given his chance by England. His game would have benefited from the experience, and he could have become an England regular for the next decade. I do not know whether it was because the recommendation came from me, an opposing captain of a national side, but the England selectors waited three more years before calling him up.

Perhaps they felt he was too aggressive, too attacking. The English selectors do not have a reputation for taking too many chances with young batsmen. They like to pick them when they are twenty-five or more and hardened to the practices of county cricket.

My West Indies colleague Deryck Murray was at Nottingham University around this time after spending two years on the staff at Trent Bridge. He later went on to play for Warwickshire, and the experience helped make him a better player.

The Nottinghamshire bowlers were all steady trusted performers, with Mike Taylor, whose twin Derek kept wicket for Somerset, perhaps the best and most reliable of the seamers. The late Barry Stead was an energetic left-arm pace bowler who was underrated. He was a good man to have on your staff, always cheerful and helpful. Dave Halfyard, the former Kent bowler, was still there. Dave was an accurate medium-pacer who hated being taken off, which explained why he usually bowled more overs than anyone else.

That first season I bowled 773 overs myself, which was a large number by today's standards. I played in 26 matches in the championship (which was a 28-match competition instead of the present 24) and took 83 wickets, a satisfactory start.

Bob 'Knocker' White was the first-choice off-spin bowler. He joined us because he had few opportunities at Middlesex with Fred Titmus on the staff and proved a consistent performer. I could always call on him when the game was tight. Another ex-Middlesex bowler on the staff was the always smiling Hary Latchman, a leg-spinner from Jamaica. In those days some counties still had leg-spinners.

I do not accept that the leg-spinner is now extinct and that there is no room for him in county cricket. There is a greater need than ever for unusual bowlers who can trick batsmen out, especially as most present-day players have no experience against this type of attack. In the fifties, most county sides had leg-spinners or slow left-hand bowlers like Jack Walsh and Denis Compton who bowled Chinamen and googlies. Most of them took a lot of wickets. Then the game in England became more defensive, and with all the restrictions about limiting overs the emphasis was put on contain-ing batsmen.

Leg-spinners were phased out. Robin Hobbs was one of the last. I would have bowled more in my Chinaman and googly style myself but for an injury in 1966 which made it virtually impossible to continue. I loved bowling in this style, especially when the ball was turning. The left-arm bowler can turn his Chinaman and off-break to a right-handed batsman far more than any off-spinner.

I remember bowling this way in one match on a turning pitch, and the ball was doing so much that the wicket-keeper was having difficulty taking it. The slip fielder – I believe it was Seymour Nurse – said to the wicket-keeper: 'You take the Chinaman and I'll go for the googly!'

During 1966 I started to feel pain when I bowled the googly, as though my shoulder was popping out of the socket. It is a common complaint among googly-bowlers. I went to see a specialist, and he told me the tendons around the shoulder had loosened over the years and an operation would cure the problem. I did not think it was worth the trouble, because by that time I was mainly bowling at my quicker pace. I could still bowl orthodox slow left-arm and the Chinaman, but the googly remained a problem. I might try a few overs and then it would go, so I had to give it up.

A promising leg-spinner who never kept bowling was Harry Pilling at Lancashire. I first met Harry when he was a fourteen-year-old tossing the ball up when I was playing for Radcliffe in the

Lancashire League. Harry became one of the characters of county cricket, playing longer than most of them. He was unlucky not to play representative cricket.

Every county side seemed to have characters. Down at Somerset, there was Bill Alley, the Australian who kept going into his fifties. Bill never stopped talking, even when he became an umpire. Greg Chappell was on the staff in those days. Unlike the rest of us, who were instantly registered, he qualified by residence, which showed his determination to get to the top.

One of the best cricketers around was Barry Knight, the Essex and England all-rounder. Barry moved the ball both ways at a lively pace and, next to Fred Trueman, probably got me out more than any other English bowler, dismissing me three times in the three-Test series in 1969. Three years earlier, he had me lbw at Lord's when I was padding up. That was a dodgy decision because the present rule which says a batsman can be out if the impact is outside the line of the stumps hadn't been adopted.

England has been looked on as the training-ground of the best of the world's cricketers because so many have played there either in League cricket or county cricket. The main reason why so many cricketers from other countries came to England was not so much to broaden their experience, although obviously they did that by playing on so many different types of pitch, as to earn a living. England is the one country where most of the cricket is professional. In the West Indies and Australia, for example, players are amateurs until they are picked for their country.

An English upbringing is good for overseas players, particularly West Indians, because it teaches them discipline and how to play the ball on its merits. Once the shine goes off the ball on Caribbean pitches batsmen can stand up and play their shots, untroubled by the conditions. But in England the ball can swing all day, or it can seam about, and a more cautious approach is demanded.

Much was expected of me when I went to Nottinghamshire and, though I did reasonably well in my first year, I felt guilty that I was not able to play for them more in subsequent seasons because of Test calls and injury. I found county cricket too taxing, almost boring in some respects. We played every day after the introduction of the John Player Sunday League, and with all the travelling there was little time to rest. A lot of matches were unrealistic because they were decided on last-day declarations and run-chases.

I suggested in 1968 that the system of three-day matches should be scrapped and replaced with four-day games, which are a better test. The players can play real cricket, not contrived cricket. In 1988 the Test and County Cricket Board started to experiment with a few four-day games, bringing them into line with other countries.

With the limit of 100 overs on the first innings, many English middle-order batsmen have to come in and play as though it was a one-day match. It was not helping their development as players. I believe one four-day match and one or occasionally two one-day matches, should be the maximum a county player should be asked to play each week. He needs a day off as much as anyone else, or a day to practise as opposed to playing. What happens now is that the young players practise among themselves. They will learn more, and quicker, if they practise with senior players.

18 | Wes Hall and a Few Other Fast Bowlers

Wes Hall was not only one of the great fast bowlers of all time but also a great character. He was one of four bowlers in my twenty years of Test cricket who would give his captain maximum effort whatever the conditions. In no special order of merit, the others were Dennis Lillee of Australia, Fred Trueman of England and Charlie Griffith, Wes's opening partner. These were the men I would rank as the top fast bowlers of my time.

They were not the fastest bowlers I played with or against. That honour goes to Roy Gilchrist, the West Indian who had a brief, controversial Test career between 1957 and 1959. I shall say more about him later. I believe he was marginally faster than the Englishman Frank Tyson who played 17 Tests between 1954 and 1959. Frank's career was also short, which seems to confirm that bowlers of extreme pace cannot sustain it for any length of time.

Wes was a tearaway when we first toured together in England in 1957, bowling so many no balls that he couldn't be risked in the Tests. But by the time we went to India and Pakistan in 1958–9 he had become a more mature bowler and took 46 wickets in the two series. I cannot recall another fast bowler taking as many wickets as that in such a short space of time in the subcontinent.

Like Fred Trueman, he was full of heart, always ready to bowl when asked, even if the pitch was flat and with little bounce. In the 1963 Test at Lord's, which was so highly lauded, he bowled non-stop for 3 hours 20 minutes. How many more wickets would he have taken in Tests if the West Indies had had four and not merely two fast bowlers in the side when he was at his peak? Considerably more than the 192 he finished up with in his ten-year career, during which he played only 48 Tests!

Nowadays the West Indian fast bowlers can be used in short spells, ensuring that they are always comparatively fresh when they return. No bowler bowls for three hours or more these days.

Wes and I had many funny experiences over the years. There was an occasion at Lord's in 1957 when, fielding on the leg side, the ball struck him on the head. He massaged his leg by mistake!

On his last tour of India in 1967–8 few of the West Indian batsmen could read the bowling of the Indian leg-break bowler B. S. Chandrasekhar, who had the marathon figures of 61.5–17–157–7 in the first innings of the First Test at the Brabourne Stadium in Bombay. In the second innings Chandra opened the bowling and sent down a further 31 overs and took 4 more wickets for 74 runs. He was supposed to be a spin bowler but in that match was India's fastest bowler!

In the Second Test in Calcutta, Wes and I came together at 290–7, and he played and missed a few times. I went down the pitch and said: 'You're playing down the wrong line. You've got to get that foot over more.'

Replied Wes: 'I thought there was something wrong.' He said he couldn't see which way the ball was going and pleaded for my help.

'I'll give you a signal,' I said. 'If it's the googly, I'll swing my bat out so.'

The ploy worked. Every time Chandra used the googly or the ball that came in from the off, because I never accepted that he bowled a proper googly, I pushed my bat out from the pad and Wes was able to plant his left leg down the line and make sure he middled the ball. This went on until tea when the stand had passed the 50 mark.

In the dressing-room during the interval I overheard Wes boasting to some of the other players how he succeeded in reading the mighty Chandra. 'It's Sobey I'm worried about,' he said. 'He can't read him.' When play resumed I decided to punish him for his impertinence and neglected to give my warning signal. Thinking the next delivery was the normal leg break, Wes tried to heave the ball to leg and was caught off the edge! 'I thought you were reading it,' I said.

In India in 1958–9, Wes and Gilchrist were feared by the Indians – they bowled so fast. The first time he kept to Gillie, wicket-keeper Gerry Alexander couldn't believe he was so quick. One or two Indian batsmen were 'absent ill' on the scorecard in that series.

Gillie hated batsmen and delighted in knocking them down. He had heard that one of the Indian batsmen, Swaranjit Singh, a left-hander who played for Cambridge University in 1954–6, had said something derogatory about him, and when they met on the field he let him have a spate of bouncers, which was acceptable, and a few beamers, which weren't. The beamer is cricket's deadliest delivery, because when aimed at the batsman it is hard to pick up and harder still to avoid. It is rightly banned, and any bowler bowling it deliberately cannot expect to have a long career.

Many bowlers have let slip a beamer in their time and have usually apologised to the batsman. Fred Trueman used to bowl the odd one on his first tour of the West Indies. But Gillie rarely said sorry: he meant it.

Gerry Alexander had also been to Cambridge University, and beamers weren't part of his cricketing philosophy. He was a highly strung, tense man who smoked up to forty cigarettes a day. He was always urging the players to greater efforts. 'C'mon,' he kept saying. He soon fell out with Gillie who, though capable of showing a fair amount of common sense on occasions, did not take too much notice of what people told him. He thought people were laughing at him which made him even madder. When Alexander told him to stop bowling beamers he ignored him.

It was a difficult situation for the captain. His best fast bowler wasn't carrying out his instructions. Discipline was stricter in those days, and Alexander decided that Gilchrist would have to go. He told the team committee that he was sending him home. The members of the committee pleaded with him to change his mind. Gilchrist was too important to the team. So Alexander relented, and Gilchrist played 4 Tests in India in which he took 26 wickets at 16 apiece.

But the arguments continued, and Alexander was adamant that Gilchrist must return to the West Indies and not be allowed to undertake the tour of Pakistan which followed. That was the end of Gillie's career: a mere 13 Tests

I played against him and sometimes with him in odd games after that when we were both League cricketers, and he remained a very quick bowler. Some of the League batsmen were petrified of him, and there were numerous occasions when he was involved in rows and was banned.

Whether it was the slow Northampton pitch which ended Frank Tyson's career or maybe his action, he had only eight years in county cricket, which is not long for a bowler of his class. More probably the reason was his action. His right knee tended to bend as he followed through. If he had had a high upright action like Michael Holding, his career would have been much longer. I played against him in the West Indies in 1956 when he toured with Jim Swanton's team and was the leading wicket-taker with 26 wickets. A man with an impressive torso, his bowling relied on brute strength more than on a classic action.

He had just returned from a triumphal tour of Australia when his 28 wickets at 20 each helped England retain the Ashes. Then he was at his peak. I reckon a fast bowler is at his best for about five or six years. Wes's peak years were between 1959 and 1966 and Fred Trueman's between 1958 and 1963.

Today's bowlers like Ian Botham have an advantage because they can play in seventy or more Tests in the five or six years they are on top and, if successful, can capture up to 300 wickets. In my opinion this has totally devalued records. Trueman's 67 Tests were spaced out between 1952 and 1965 and Wes's 48 between 1959 and 1969.

Botham shares with Trueman the ability to make the batsman think he is doing something extraordinary when often he isn't. When Trueman was bowling, you never knew what to expect next. Early on in his career he would sometimes try a beamer. That was before he became respectable!

Fred always had something to say. If he beat you, he would say: 'Too good for you, sunshine.' He was abusive with it but never, in my experience, in an offensive manner. He was a character and we accepted him as such. He was popular in the West Indies.

I remember once lifting a bouncer from him into the stand in Barbados, and he stood, hands on hips, and said: 'That were a ————— good bouncer and a bloody good shot.' After that I noticed he did not bowl many bouncers at me.

On his home pitch in Perth, Dennis Lillee was as quick as anyone and, like Trueman, he taught himself to be a better bowler once the sharp edge of his youthful pace disappeared. They were very similar as people – great triers, cussers and generous-hearted men who would applaud batsmen who got the better of them. Not so much on the field, but over a drink afterwards. Fred tried to prolong his career by playing Sunday cricket with Derbyshire in his early forties. Lillee is seeking to do the same by coming out of retirement at the age of thirty-eight.

I have already written at length about Charlie Griffith, a bowler whose determination was a great asset to the West Indies side between 1959 and 1969. A less mentally strong character would have quit when all the agitation was going on about his bowling action between 1962 and 1967. It affected him badly. He thought everyone was against him, but he kept going and he answered his critics on the field. Fast bowling is as much about mental attitude as about strength, fitness and technique.

Charlie didn't only intimidate English, Australian and Indian batsmen. Some of his fellow West Indians were not too keen to face him, either, at his most ferocious.

When the Shell Shield started in 1966 and Barbados won it in the first year, a strong Guyanese team came to Bridgetown to play a Barbados side that contained no less than ten Test players. Guyana had an outstanding batting side in those days with players like Steve Camacho, Rohan Kanhai, Basil Butcher, Joe Solomon and Clive Lloyd, and on a good batting pitch Charlie routed them with figures of 3–28 and 4–49.

In the second innings he removed openers Camacho and Vincent Mayers with fearsome bouncers and was bowling so fast that only Kanhai and Lloyd, who showed what a great player he was developing into by scoring 107, seemed to have the will to take him on. Basil Butcher, one of the best West Indian batsmen, was struck on the pad first ball and without waiting for the umpire's decision walked off. It was the only time I had seen a batsman walk for an lbw. Basil had made 99 in the first innings but didn't fancy Charlie in that mood!

I was often asked which bowler, or type of bowling, gave me most problems. Was it Fred, or Dennis Lillee who once gave me such a torrid time in Australia that I was glad to be dismissed, or my own Barbadian team mates Wes and Charlie when I played against them in club matches? I would not say that there was anyone in particular. All batsmen are vulnerable to the first few deliveries they face, no matter how good they are.

That was what made Brian Close's decision to field so close at short leg at the Oval in 1966 such a match-winning tactic. I was scoring runs almost at will in that series, and Mike Smith and Colin Cowdrey, who preceded Close as England captain, usually put the field back when I came in. Close recognised the basic cricketing truth that all players, no matter how many runs they scored in their last few innings, are liable to get out early. Once I got in, I believed I was no more susceptible to pace or spin or any type of bowling. Fast bowling was a challenge which I enjoyed taking up, unless of course the pitch was substandard.

Most batsmen find more trouble with the ball leaving the bat than with the one coming in. A good player who will be looking to play it will probably get a nick. A bad player will miss it. I have already said that Alan Davidson, the Australian left-hander, was an opponent I respected greatly but, being a left-hander, his stock ball usually came in, which made it easier. It was the one which went the other way which I found more bothersome!

My most memorable contest with Davidson came in 1961–2 when I was playing for South Australia. The success of the West Indies tour earlier that year brought invitations to Wes Hall, Rohan Kanhai and myself to play in the Sheffield Shield, and we became the first overseas players to take part in the competition. I did not do so well in my first year, but in my second and third years I became the first player to do the double of 1000 runs and 50 wickets, and eventually South Australia won the Shield for the first time in ten years.

As there were only five other teams competing in the Sheffield Shield in those days it was no mean feat to do the double. I was as proud of that achievement as I was of my Test records. Having been one of the few cricketers to have played in the Shell Shield in the West Indies, the Sheffield Shield in Australia and the English county championship – Rohan Kanhai, Andy Roberts, Viv Richards, Joel Garner and Michael Holding were among the others – I can say that the standard in the Sheffield Shield in Australia is the highest of the three. The leading cricketers are concentrated in six (Tasmania made the sixth) teams, which means the overall standard is higher than in England where the talent is spread among seventeen teams. Perhaps in recent years the quality of the fast bowling in the West Indies might have made the standard in the Shell Shield comparable, or even better. There is not much to choose between the two forms of cricket. Both are highly competitive.

My last match for South Australia in 1962 was against the strongest side of the day, New South Wales. Richie Benaud was the New South Wales captain, and he had a side of Test strength under his command, with players of the calibre of Bobby Simpson, Ian Craig, Neil Harvey, Norman O'Neill, Brian Booth, Graeme Thomas, Alan Davidson, Johnny Martin and Frank Misson, all Test players. We had some Test players of our own, including Les Favell, Neil Hawke, Barry Jarman, Rex Sellers and David Sincock.

Davidson bowled us out for 190 in the first innings with 5–40. I took 9 wickets in the match and scored 251 in the second innings, enabling us to inflict the first defeat of the season on Benaud's team. The match was at the Adelaide Oval, a peculiarly shaped ground with short boundaries to the side of the wicket and extremely long ones behind the arms of the bowlers. I have seen a batsman run a five on a straight hit where the boundaries are up to 110 yards.

I was around 150 when Davo, who had dismissed me twice in three innings already that season, took the second new ball. The first delivery was a beamer that came straight at my head – the most menacing delivery, I think, I ever had bowled at me. I just managed to get my bat up in time, and the ball flashed through the slips for four. Davo rushed up and apologised, claiming the ball had slipped from his hand.

Two overs later he bowled a bouncer, and I got into position early and slapped it with a flat bat from outside the off stump. The ball sailed on and on, straight down the ground. The carry must have been 150 yards. I had never hit a ball that far before and never managed to do it again. I will always cherish that shot, more especially as I might not have been around to play it if Davo's beamer had caught me in the head instead of the back of my bat.

Like all fast bowlers – Trueman, Lillee, Griffith and Wes – he had a fiery temper at times. It's part of a fast bowler's weaponry to feel hostile to batsmen. When I arrived back in Adelaide a year later, I met Col Egar, who had been umpiring in that match. 'You know, Garry,' he said, 'I don't believe that Davo's beamer slipped. When he passed me on his way back to his mark, he said: "I'll show him a thing or two!"'

19 | Leading the World XI

The best I bowled in England in the summer of 1970 was at Headingley in the Fourth Test in the Rest of the World series. Yet I failed to take a wicket! It was a good example of how much a bowler relies on luck. Some days it happens for him. Other days it doesn't.

England's best defensive batsman, Geoff Boycott, was batting along with the gritty Kent opener Brian Luckhurst. I beat the bat three or four times an over. 'You're doing too much,' said Boycott. I bowled 20 overs and conceded 24 runs. After putting England in on a damp pitch, we should have bowled them out cheaply, but they managed to reach 222, with Keith Fletcher showing promise in his 89.

The ball usually swings at Headingley on at least one day of a five-day match. I don't know why this is. Perhaps it is because it is usually damper in the North! Headingley is the one ground in England where it is always useful to have a swing bowler. I managed to score 114 in that match, and the World team won by 2 wickets.

The team was brought together to stand in for the South Africans, whose tour had been cancelled on the advice of the British government following the rejection by the South African Prime Minister of Basil d'Oliveira in the England side to tour his country. I believe it was the strongest collection of cricketers ever assembled in England, yet despite containing great players like Graeme Pollock, Barry Richards, Mike Procter, Rohan Kanhai, Lance Gibbs and Clive Lloyd we struggled to beat a moderate England side. There were occasions when we had to rely on the number eleven batsman, Intikhab Alam, to score a few runs.

There were no problems about motivation, and it could not be said that the players were slacking. The series was sponsored by Guinness, who put up a £13,000 prize fund which was split £2000 for each Test victory and £3000 for the side winning the rubber. As the World XI won 4–1, we shared £11,000 among the fourteen-man squad. In those days Test match fees were modest. It was a considerable sum to play for, and the matches were fought out in a competitive spirit.

I was reluctant to accept the invitation to lead the side, because I felt it was unfair I should desert my county, Nottinghamshire, for half the summer. But the Test and County Cricket Board put pressure on me, saying that if I didn't take the job I would not be allowed to play for Nottinghamshire. I was not happy about that but could do little about it. The counties shared some of the proceeds of the series, so Nottinghamshire did not lose out financially.

Before the first match, I asked whether the matches would be Test status and if the averages would count in the normal Test averages. I was told that that was the case. It would have proved difficult to find sponsors otherwise. At the end of the series, I learned that the matches had not been official Tests as Tests are traditionally played by country against country. So my average of 73 from 588 runs, one of my more profitable returns, didn't count. Nor did my 21 wickets at 21 apiece.

I do not know why some of the World XI players did not perform as well as expected. Graeme Pollock, for instance, did not score a hundred until the final Test. England only had one fast bowler, John Snow, but Pollock did not look entirely happy against him. Pollock's South African colleague Barry Richards also disappointed. Barry made stacks of runs in county cricket but, whether it was because he didn't find the series stimulating enough or maybe it was a lapse in form, he failed to live up to his reputation.

If a batsman is capable of scoring a century, he owes it to his team to score one as often as he can. The attitude of saying to oneself, 'If I don't get a score, it doesn't matter because we've got a lot of good players to come,' is totally unprofessional, but I suspect that some of my players felt that way.

At number six in the order, I should not have been required on many occasions. But I batted in every Test twice except for the First Test at Lord's where I scored 183 in the World team's 546.

I took 6–21 in the first innings at Lord's, in terms of figures one of the best spells of my career. But I did not bowl as well as I did in Leeds. I asked the England side to bat in humid conditions, and the ball swung a long way.

I always liked bowling at Lord's. It was second to Headingley as the ground in England which helped swing bowling. I remember one delivery which left Basil d'Oliveira stranded. It started to come in through the air and left him off the pitch. Basil was in a technically sound position, bat tight against the body, but the ball found the edge and Faroukh Engineer made the catch. Basil left with a rueful expression on his face.

Swing bowlers have to pitch the ball further up, because if they drop it short the swing starts too early and the batsman can react. So there was never any question of me taking advantage of the ridge in that match. The experts say there is a slight incline at the Nursery End which, despite remedial work, still remains. It is supposed to be on a fast bowler's length. I never knew much about it myself.

There are times in a bowler's life when he recognises that he is close to perfection. That happened to me at Lord's, and it was a pleasurable feeling.

The fastest bowler in the World XI attack was the South African Mike Procter. He ran in fast and bowled off the wrong foot at a very rapid pace. His action meant he swung the ball into the bat, but the odd delivery went straight through. He made the ball zip off the pitch. I played against him when he was with Gloucestershire and rated him an all-rounder of world class.

The England team had a bowler nearly as fast in their ranks, Derbyshire's Alan Ward, but Alan never seemed to be fully fit. Eddie Barlow, not as quick as Procter or Ward, turned out to be our most successful wicket-taker. I wouldn't rank him among the top bowlers of the day, yet he had so much enthusiasm and competitive spirit that he often succeeded where better bowlers had failed. He would make the batsmen think he was doing something even if he wasn't. Most good bowlers do that. Fred Trueman was an outstanding example.

The World team would have won more easily if Ray Illingworth, the England captain, had surrendered his wicket with less of a fight. Illingworth proved himself an all-rounder of some class with scores of 63, 94, 15, 43, 58, 54, 52 and 0. He played straight, took no risks and defied the bowlers to get him out.

The Rest of the World team that took on Australia in 1971–2, again in place of a banned South African tour, was much weaker. Our biggest handicap was not having a fast bowler to counter Dennis Lillee. A recent arrival on the Test scene, Dennis was twenty-two, and I don't think he has bowled any quicker than he did in that series.

I was hoping to have a rest before playing a few matches for South Australia when Sir Donald Bradman rang me and asked if I wanted to lead the World XI. I was reluctant, but Sir Donald is a persuasive man and I agreed to take the job.

I first saw Dennis in the opening representative match in Brisbane, which ended in a draw. I was sitting with Ray Lindwall, and after Dennis bowled his first delivery I turned to him and said: 'Does this fellow have to take such a long run?' The next ball I discovered why: it was extremely fast and soared towards Rodney Marsh some twenty yards back past a bemused Hylton Ackerman.

A South African who played for Northamptonshire in the English county championship, Hylton wasn't a bad player but he wasn't in this class.

'If this boy Lillee can work up this pace on a slow pitch, what's he going to do in Perth, which is a fast wicket?' I said to Ray.

'Just wait and see,' he replied.

When we arrived at the WACA ground in December Richard Hutton and I went to inspect the pitch. It was rock hard. Richard had a ball with him and bounced it in the middle. The ball bounced back up and nearly hit him in the head. 'When I do that at Headingley I've got to get a shovel to dig it out,' he said.

Australia made 349, and when our innings was due to start the next morning I noticed there was still some dampness left in the pitch. Sunny Gavaskar and Faroukh Engineer opened. Lillee's first ball passed over Sunny's head, and Marsh just managed to reach it. The next ball took off and went in the same direction off a length.

In the dressing-room there were signs of panic among the World players. 'Don't anyone ask to go down the order because that's where I'm going,' I said. 'I'm an old man.' Sunny went to a Marsh catch off Dennis, and Faroukh started to back away to leg. Soon he was spooning an easy return catch to Lillee. 'Well bowled,' he said as he left the scene.

I went in at 46–5, and I can honestly say that was the only occasion in my career when I felt a little anxious about my physical wellbeing. Normally fast bowling did not worry me. I loved the challenge. But here was possibly the fastest bowler I had faced on the world's fastest pitch, which was giving him a great deal of assistance.

The first delivery was very fast and went through to Marsh without me having time to play a shot even if I had wanted to. I turned to Rod, and he shrugged his shoulders as if to say there was nothing he could do about it. The next ball, straighter, also took off and hit my glove on the way to the wicket-keeper. I was never so pleased to be out. 'Thanks very much,' I said to Rod. The World team were bowled out in a mere 14.1 overs, little more than an hour and a half, for a paltry 59. Dennis's figures were 7.1–3–29–8. Rohan Kanhai made a brilliant century in the second innings, but we still lost by an innings and 11 runs.

We were heavily criticised in the press by critics who accused us of being unprofessional and not trying. As captain, I bore the brunt of it. I was determined we would perform better in the third match, starting in Melbourne on New Year's Day. In my time playing for South Australia, Melbourne was the only major ground in Australia where I had not made a century. Our first innings followed the same pattern as at Perth. Lillee soon rattled out Gavaskar and Ackerman, and Bob Massie, potentially one of Australia's finest swing bowlers, had Zaheer Abbass caught.

It was one of cricket's greatest mysteries why Massie blew out so quickly. He looked a good bowler in that match and proved it at Lord's the following year when he took 16–137 against England, the best analysis by any bowler at the ground. He played only 6 Tests in all and went back to club cricket, where he started.

We were 26–3 when I went to the crease to face Lillee. First ball, a short one, I played too soon, and Keith Stackpole caught me at ankle height in the slips. In Australia, players usually have a beer with the opposing team, and later on I was chatting to Ian Chappell, the Australian captain.

'What's up with this fellow Lillee?' I said. 'I've met him in three innings now, and every time he's let me have a bouncer first up. Tell him I can bowl them, too!'

I was bowling when Lillee, the Australian number eleven, came in to bat. I hadn't thought of letting him have a bouncer, but Tony Greig, in his typically aggressive way, shouted from mid-on: 'Let him have it, let him have the bouncer.' So I bowled a bouncer which whizzed past Dennis's nose, and it had him rattled. Next ball he made a poor shot, and Bishen Bediu caught him at mid-off.

Dennis was furious when he returned to the dressing-room. Ian Chappell told me later he said: 'I'll teach that cheeky bastard a lesson! I haven't bowled flat out at him yet.' The World XI were in a healthier position when I came out at 146–3 in the second innings. Once more Lillee, whose first-innings figures were 5–48, had the ball.

Anticipating that I would be expecting a bouncer, he bowled a well pitched-up delivery which I straight drove for four off the middle of the bat. In his first three overs, I struck 29. Everything went right for me. Nearly every shot found the gaps, and my century came up in 129 deliveries. Peter Pollock, the South African bowler who had a miserable tour with the ball, helped me put on 186 for the eighth wicket. If I had come close to perfection bowling at Lord's in 1970, this was probably as near to perfection as I ever came with the bat.

A crowd of 50,000 saw me pass 200 and then 250 before falling to Greg Chappell at 254. Sir Donald Bradman said it was the best innings he had seen in Australia and compared it with the 232 scored by his old partner and team mate Stan McCabe at Trent Bridge in 1938.

The compliment I remember most vividly came from Dennis Lillee. As I walked past him back to the dressing-room he said: 'You know, I've read about you and now I've really seen you. We got our backsides cut good and proper today, and I still appreciate it.' That said a lot about his sportsmanship. We have been friends ever since.

20 | My Trip to Rhodesia

Near the end of the Rest of the World series in England in 1970, Eddie Barlow suggested I might like to take part in a double-wicket tournament in Rhodesia, the former British territory whose government had broken away from Britain and made a unilateral declaration of independence. I asked for a day or so to think it over and, after being told that Rhodesia was not practising apartheid like its neighbour South Africa, I decided to accept the invitation.

The Rhodesian football team was all black at the time, and I was told there was no discrimination against anyone on the grounds of colour in the selection of teams. If I had known the furore my visit was to cause, I would not have gone. For two months the issue was on the front, inside and back page of nearly every newspaper in the Caribbean. I realise, looking back, that I should have consulted with some senior officials of the West Indies Board to see how they viewed it.

But at the time we were just concluding a multi-racial Test series in England, where West Indians, Indians and Pakistanis were playing cricket together and sharing the same facilities as South Africans. We were friends in a common cause – cricket. I was as friendly with Graeme Pollock, Eddie Barlow, Mike Procter and Barry Richards as I was with Mushtaq Mohammad, Intikhab Alam and Faroukh Engineer. The various cricketing boards around the world had agreed to England playing such a team because the South Africans had been invited as individuals. They were not representing their country.

I knew nothing of the politics at the time except that the tour of England by South Africa had been cancelled for political reasons. I was a professional cricketer and I had been invited as an individual to play in a weekend tournament in Salisbury, now Harare. I was in Harare less than forty-eight hours.

The row over my visit erupted on 7 September when it was reported from London that I was going at the invitation of the Mashonaland Cricket Association. Five days later Frank Walcott, general secretary of the Barbados Workers' Union and a former first-class umpire, criticised the visit, saying: 'Mr Sobers is an international personality and represents the heart and soul of millions of people in the West Indies who see their national identity manifested in cricket and their symbol of pride and equality with nations in Garry Sobers. He cannot lapse into any area which is an offence to the dignity and character of West Indians.'

I was paid about £600 for taking part in the tournament, which was a lot of money in those days. My partner was Dr Ali Bacher, the former South African captain and now director of cricket in that country. We failed to win, which was not surprising since I stepped straight off the aircraft, had a few hours' rest and went straight to the ground.

Later I met Prime Minister Ian Smith and I remember he was most convincing when talking about outside pressures on his regime.

Peter Short, secretary of the West Indies Board of Control, issued a statement saying that the decision was mine and had nothing to do with the Board. On my arrival back at Seawell Airport, now Sir Grantley Adams Airport, in Barbados, it seemed that nearly every media man in the Caribbean was there to greet me.

I tried to explain why I had gone. 'I thought at first it would be a very good thing for me,' I said. 'I am a cricketer and I think personally of cricket, not politics. I thought that to go to Rhodesia would possibly do some good, considering the problems they had with the South African team not coming to England.'

Asked about Ian Smith, I replied: 'I thought he was a tremendous man to talk to.' That innocent comment was soon to be condemned and used against me! I was mistaken if I thought that press conference would be the end of the affair.

The *Workers Voice* newspaper of Antigua called me 'a white, black man'. The *Antigua Star* said: 'His deed was a most unkind cut to all those dedicated to the struggle against racism in all its forms.' In Guyana the newspapers called for me to be replaced as West Indies captain.

One of the few writers to appreciate my position was Brunell Jones. Writing in the *Sunday Guardian* of Trinidad, Brunell said: 'He went to Rhodesia in the honest belief he would be striking a blow for integration. Some of us might not have decided to take this line of action but the least his tormentors could have done was to respect the man's judgement, even if they did not agree with it.'

My old cricketing friend Conrad Hunte came up with an original line. Interviewed in Bombay, Conrad said: 'The question of the utmost importance is whether Sobers changes Ian Smith or the Rhodesian Prime Minister changes him.'

A week after my return Hector Wynter, Jamaica's Minister for State and Youth and Community Development, made a speech in which he said I had done an injustice to myself and to the West Indies. The issue grew into a major political row on 10 October when Forbes Burnham, Prime Minister of Guyana, said I would no longer be welcome in his country. This was a serious matter: the West Indies played a Test match in Georgetown every series. Mr Burnham had been to a meeting of ministers abroad and had been chided about 'one of his blood brothers acting as ambassador for Ian Smith'. Mr Burnham, whom I knew reasonably well, said: 'If he doesn't recant and apologise for his foolish and ill-advised stand, he will not be welcome here.' Next day, Kenny Wishart, President of the Guyana Cricket Board of Control, called for me to apologise. Peter Short commented that there was no reason to apologise.

Cameron Tudors, the Barbados Deputy Prime Minister, criticised the stand taken by Forbes Burnham. 'To say, as some say who should know better, that he would not be welcomed in their country is an affront to the people of Barbados,' he said. The West Indies Board announced they were asking clarification of Mr Burnham's statement. Did it really mean what it said?

Nearly every politician in the Caribbean was joining in. Dr Cheddi Jagan's Progressive Party in Guyana called for my resignation, and Burnham told the West Indies Board that he was demanding an apology. My house was besieged by people, one of whom was a priest who felt I might need his services! Most of the many letters in the newspapers sided with me.

The affair took another serious turn on 14 October when the ruling Labour Party in Jamaica passed a resolution requesting me to resign as West Indies captain. Michael Manley, leader of the opposition People's National Party, said that unless there was an apology 'he may not be welcomed anywhere by people who believe that justice is bigger even than sport'. I knew Michael Manley well. I'd spoken to him on many occasions and, like most West Indians, he was a cricket-lover. So much so that he has written several books on the subject, including a history of West Indies cricket.

On 19 October Peter Short confirmed that Mr Burnham was remaining firm on his stance that if no apology was forthcoming I would not be allowed into his country. In Trinidad a few days later, Vernon Jamadar, leader of the opposition, praised what he called 'Garry's calm dignity in response to the primitive savagery of West Indian gutter politicians'.

Support was also coming for me in Barbados. Lionel Craig, an opposition MP, late Deputy Premier, tabled a resolution calling on the House to deplore Burnham's statement. There was a suggestion, not taken up, that I should be invited to open the country's new national stadium instead of Prince Charles.

Dr Eric Williams, Prime Minister of Trinidad, then stepped in and spoke to Wes Hall, who in turn came to see me to explain the views of the Trinidadian Prime Minister. Dr Williams said that he had spoken to Mrs Indira Gandhi, Prime Minister of India, about the possible effect on the coming tour of the West Indies by the Indian team. It was being suggested that the tour might have to be called off.

I couldn't believe that a weekend trip to Rhodesia could cause such problems. Around this time I received a telephone call from the Barbados Prime Minister, Mr Errol Barrow, from New York where he was to address the United Nations General Assembly. Mr Barrow seemed to know all the facts and asked me to do nothing until he returned. He told me he and most of the other governments knew I planned to go and should have advised me of their opposition before I left.

When he arrived back in Barbados, he told me that the crisis could be solved if I issued a statement which, if properly worded, would pacify the critics, Mr Burnham in particular. He drafted the letter himself, and I signed it. It was addressed to the President of the West Indies Board of Control and said:

> Dr Mr President,
>
> When I accepted an invitation to take part in a two day, double wicket competition in Rhodesia I was assured that there was no segregation in sport in that country but I was not made aware of the deep feelings of the West Indies people. I have since learnt of this feeling and the wider international issues involved.
>
> I am naturally deeply distressed by and concerned over the tremendous controversy and bitterness which have arisen after my return from Salisbury. As I was not aware of the serious repercussions I may have expressed myself in such a way as to create the impression of indifference to these issues.
>
> Mr President, I wish to inform you in all sincerity that this is far from my true feelings as the prestige of West Indian cricket and the unity and dignity of the West Indians and African people are interests I have always served.
>
> I therefore wish to convey to you and the members of the Board my sincere regrets for any embarrassment which my action may have caused and assure you of my unqualified dedication whenever I may be called upon to represent my country, the West Indies, and my people.
>
> G. St A. Sobers

Mr Barrow, known to his friends as 'Skipper', was a wonderful man. Any Barbadian, whether rich or poor, could call him personally with a problem and he would help them.

Two days later Mr Burnham welcomed my statement and said I would now be assured of a great welcome in his country. Mr Barrow corrected a BBC report that I had made an apology. 'The Board never demanded an apology of Mr Sobers,' he said. 'If it had,

I would find it difficult to comprehend the basis on which an apology could be demanded by the Board or anybody else.'

The Indian tour went ahead as scheduled, and I duly played in Georgetown. I was given a good reception and became the first West Indies batsman to pass 7000 Test runs when I scored 108 not out in the second innings against the Indians. That was what I was interested in: cricket. I never wanted to involve myself in politics. The problem of South Africa remains in cricket, and I cannot see a solution to it.

During my career I had a number of invitations to visit South Africa, including one from Eddie Barlow. I turned them all down.

21 | Fielding

In my day the players used to practise fielding for ten minutes or so before the start of play. Today the practice can last up to an hour. It is one feature of the game which has improved out of all recognition. We took around 50 per cent of the chances that came our way. Today, with so much money riding on the outcome of matches, that has increased to 75 per cent or more.

It is always said that 'catches win matches', and I know it is true, as I have mentioned, because I skippered a losing side in Australia once because we dropped 34 catches in 5 Tests. When you drop a batsman, you give him another innings.

I fielded either at short leg, very close, or at second slip. I have already explained why I fielded so close on the leg side, particularly to the bowling of Lance Gibbs. If I had to nominate a catch which pleased me more than any other, it was perhaps the one in Australia in the 1960–1 series when I dived forward at second slip and caught the great Australian left-hander Neil Harvey, dislocating my finger as I did so. Neil was a player whom you never gave an extra innings.

A fielder who deliberately fields closer than the textbooks recommend in today's game is Ian Botham. Ian usually stands a couple of yards ahead of the rest of the slip cordon, and it has enabled him to pick up many low catches which would not have carried if he had been standing further back. Until recently, his record has been tremendous, but as he has passed thirty his reflexes have slowed. I do not think he helps himself by the way he stands, often with his hands on his knees. A slip fielder should be crouching, with his hands held close to the ground because it is far easier to come up than it is to go down.

I preferred second slip, where you watch the outside edge of the bat, because I was free to go both sides. I loved diving. I reckoned I was pretty agile: a legacy of my days as a goalkeeper. At first slip you are sometimes less keen to go to the left, because the wicket-keeper is there with his gloves and you might decide to leave it to him.

Most of the great slip fielders stand at first slip, and the two leading exponents in my day were Australia's Bobby Simpson and England's Phil Sharpe. Colin Cowdrey wasn't bad, either. Bobby had an individualistic style: he used to like to clutch the ball into his body when he caught it to prevent it bouncing out.

Sharpe, now an England selector, was such a good catcher that his catching prowess almost got him into the side. Given a choice between him and a good batsman who was not such a good fielder, the selectors sometimes went for him, and he justified their faith against the West Indies in 1966.

One of the top West Indian slip fielders was Robin Bynoe of Barbados. Robin was selected for a tour of India in 1959 and ignored until he went on another tour there in 1967–8.

Too frequently in the past politics has played a part in the selection of the West Indies side, and a number of good players were excluded for non-cricketing reasons. Robin had a fine Shell Shield before the squad was picked for the 1966 tour of England, and I thought he would be a certainty. I believed I had the support of the selectors, but at the meeting they spoke against Bynoe and for Joey Carew, Easton McMorris and Steve Camacho. None of them was as good as Bynoe. I think some of them felt he was too lackadaisical because he liked skylarking.

At that same meeting I wanted Clive Lloyd to be included and was voted down. They preferred the left-handed all rounder Rawle Brancker. These days the captain is more powerful and usually gets his way at selection meetings. That was not the case twenty or more years ago.

Clive was one of the greatest all-rounder fielders the West Indies have ever possessed. In his younger days he was so quick and agile in the covers that it was dangerous to go for a run when the ball was anywhere near him. He was a tremendous thrower, though not in the same class as the South African Colin Bland, universally accepted as the greatest thrower of my time or any other time.

I was present in Adelaide when Clive seriously injured his back making a miraculous attempt to catch a full-blooded cover drive which was never more than two feet off the ground. He ran across and must have dived six or seven yards as he got his left hand to the ball. Unfortunately he twisted his back as he fell and was forced to spend some time in hospital. I do not believe he was as fit afterwards as he was before the incident.

Bland used to put on fielding and throwing demonstrations lasting up to half an hour. He told me he practised daily and could hit the stumps from the most difficult of angles. He had a flat powerful throw which would home in on the stumps even when he was off balance.

The Australian Paul Sheahan was another spectacular cover fielder, though not in the class of Lloyd or Bland. Today's equivalent in the West Indies side is the Trinidadian Gus Logie, who has saved countless runs in his time in the Test arena.

My former Nottinghamshire team mate Derek Randall was the first player I can recall sliding into the line of the ball close to the boundary and dragging it back with his foot. Soon players around the world were copying him and it became an accepted part of the out-fielder's repertoire.

The advent of one-day cricket has made out-fielding, or sweeping the boundary, a very important part of the game, and most sides these days have fielders who can dive full length to prevent fours.

Every run counted in my day, but these days it counts more in terms of cash and bonuses. Many of the one-day matches are now decided by the most slender of margins, and the losers can often look back to a brilliant piece of fielding which denied them, or a less brilliant example of their own fielding.

In my time, most fast bowlers used to field at deep fine leg or third man to give them a rest between overs. Charlie Griffith always used to field in the deep. In the modern West Indies side some of the best catchers in the slips and gully have been the fast bowlers – Michael

Holding and Joel Garner, like me an ex-goalkeeper, among them. The modern fast bowler has no time to relax.

Two Indian players in my earlier days who were brilliant shot-stoppers were Gaekwad and Adhikari. They perfected the art of flicking the ball up into their hand and throwing in on the run. And they could do it against the hardest of drives from the bats of Everton Weekes and Clyde Walcott, both powerful strikers of the ball.

Most successful teams had good fielders. Ian Chappell was one of the best slip fielders I saw and he rarely dropped chances. His brother Greg was also a good catcher.

These days it is possible to stand close to the bat protected by a helmet with visor, shin-pads and arm-pads. I do not think that is right. If a fielder wants to stand close, he should accept the risk. Brian Close always did and was never hurt. Being heavily protected gives the fielder an unfair advantage.

It is difficult to say who was the best wicket-keeper I played with or against. I believe you should select your best wicket-keeper. If he can also bat, then the team benefits. Too many English wicket-keepers have been chosen because they were good batsmen and fair wicket-keepers. Keith Andrew and Bob Taylor were probably the leading English wicket-keepers in my day, yet both played fewer Tests than they deserved because their batting was not up to Test standard. Surrey's Roy Swetman, for instance, was once preferred on a tour of the West Indies to the admirable Andrew.

Afterwards, Jim Parks, a batsman of genuine Test class, toured the West Indies as first-choice wicket-keeper, though few people would agree that he was England's best wicket-keeper at that time. Bob Taylor was unlucky to be in competition with Alan Knott for much of his career. Alan was a great wicket-keeper and a run-scorer. Some of my English friends tell me Godfrey Evans was the best of them all in England, but I did not see enough of him to make a judgement.

Some wicket-keepers throw themselves about acrobatically, and that does not appeal to me. I prefer the quiet efficient wicket-keepers whose positioning and anticipation are sound. Gil Langley, the Australian, was in that mould, and I remember seeing him make a tremendous catch down the leg side off a leg glide by Frank Worrell.

He made it look so easy I was certain that most people in the ground did not appreciate the outstanding quality of the catch. The late Wally Grout was similar in style to Gil. Neither of them missed much. Rod Marsh was one of the best wicket-keepers I saw against fast bowlers, but you rarely saw him against the slow bowlers and that has to be one of the supreme tests of a keeper. Among the Indians, the better performers behind the stumps were Faroukh Engineer, the bald-headed Kirmani and the underrated Kunderan.

22 | Time to Quit

In twenty years of Test cricket during which I played 87 consecutive Tests and 93 in all, I played on a number of occasions when I was not fully fit. There was an occasion at Leeds which I have related when I had a painful whitlow lanced the day before a Test and a doctor advised me not to play. Sir Frank Worrell said the team needed me, so I turned out. Every time I played a shot against Fred Trueman's bowling, I was in pain. There were other times when I had slight muscle strains, sore fingers and an aching left knee.

My knee deteriorated to such an extent that when I had a second operation on it in 1972 the surgeon said he was amazed that I could still play cricket. The bones were rubbing against each other and flaking away. The left knee was the one that took the strain when I bowled. My full weight was on it as I swivelled round. It is not the landing leg which bears the brunt of fast bowling, but the pivoting leg.

I suppose the joint first began to be affected when I played football as a boy. I had my first operation on my left knee in 1962 when I was playing for Radcliffe. The surgeon was a gentleman by the name of Sir Reginald Watson-Jones. I played my first season for South Australia in the Sheffield Shield that year, and playing on hard pitches may well have caused the trouble. That was when I established a record in the competition by passing 50 wickets and scoring more than 1000 runs in the same season, the first player to do so. I enjoyed playing cricket in Australia and made many friends there.

By the time the other cartilage was removed ten years later I was limping slightly and realised that not only would I not be able to play a full season for Nottinghamshire, but also I would be doubtful for the series against Australia in the West Indies early in 1973. I was thirty-six, and years of playing cricket almost all year round had taken their toll. The West Indies Board usually pays the air fare of West Indian professionals in England who are wanted for home Test series, and I contacted Cecil Marley, President of the West Indies board, and warned him that I might not be fit.

'It would not be fair to accept the Board's offer to pay my passage home,' I said. 'I might get out there and not be able to play. I'll pay my own passage. In the circumstances, I resign as captain.'

I was asked who I thought should take over. My first nomination was David Holford, because I felt he was the best captain in the West Indies. Second, I named Clive Lloyd of Guyana. He was a good enough player, and the West Indies needed to be looking to the future. My third choice was Rohan Kanhai, because he had been a loyal servant and deserved some recognition. Rohan Kanhai was appointed.

I returned home to Barbados and, working with weights, gradually built up the muscles around my knee. After my initial reservations I was now keen to play because after playing against Australia for the Rest of the World a year before I knew their players and their strengths. I wanted to face Dennis Lillee on my own pitches. When interviewed about the prospects in the coming series, I said I thought the Australians would win. I said Lillee was one of the quickest bowlers to come to the Caribbean.

This was taken by some people as being disloyal, but when asked for my views about cricket I am always frank. What I forecast happened. Even without Lillee, who broke down with a serious back injury, the Australians still won with the awkward-looking Max Walker taking most of the wickets in Lillee's place. Max, or 'Tangles' as he was known because of his odd approach to the crease, wasn't fast and he bowled inswingers off the front foot. He was particularly difficult to play if you were left-handed.

Two weeks before the First Test in Jamaica, Clyde Walcott, one of the selectors, called me and asked how I was progressing. I said that the knee was becoming stronger each day and that I felt I might be able to play in the Second Test if required.

First, I said, I would have to give it a test, and as Barbados were playing their final match in Trinidad in the Shell Shield that was an ideal opportunity. Barbados needed to win to retain the Shield. David Holford confirmed that I was wanted, and I opened the bowling and convinced myself that my knee could stand up to the rigours of a five-day Test. I bowled out twenty overs in the game and scored a few runs in each innings. It was a satisfactory test.

When the surgeon saw me after the second operation he warned me that the knee would puff up and be a little stiff, and that is what happened. But he also said there was nothing to worry about and it would soon settle down again. After the match Jeffrey Stollmeyer, chairman of the selectors, came into the dressing-room and asked: 'How's it going Garry? Any after-effects?' I explained the position and said I thought I would be ready for the Second Test in Barbados in two weeks' time.

Stollmeyer said the Board wanted me to play for Barbados against the Australians the following week to make absolutely sure about my fitness. I replied that I did not think that was necessary. I knew myself what my state of fitness was and didn't want to risk it. 'Give a young player a chance,' I said. 'I am not on trial. The selectors know what I can do.'

Stollmeyer said that if I didn't play the selectors might consider that I was not available for the Test match. They would ask the Board's doctor to conduct a fitness test. I lost my temper. I had worked hard to regain fitness, and now they wouldn't take my word for it. When I had fitness problems before Test matches in the past they would say they needed me, and I accepted that and went out and played.

No one insisted on seeing a doctor then. When people want to shirk, that's when they go to a doctor, to get him to say they aren't fit to play. No doctor could tell me about my fitness. I knew myself whether I was able to play or not. I hadn't missed a single Test for eighteen years, and they must have known I had to play sometimes when no doctor would have passed me fit.

Back home in Barbados, I went along to watch the Australian match – the Chappell brothers scored 300 in three hours – and met Clyde Walcott. Clyde said the Board still wanted me to play in the Test series and asked me to play in a two-day practice match with the rest of the squad in St Vincent. Once more, they were putting me on trial, doubting my word. I am afraid I was rude to Clyde. 'You know where to put your trial game,' I stormed.

I never played in that series against the Australians. Towards the end of their tour, a limited-overs tournament was held in Barbados for my benefit fund. Organised by Banks, the brewery in the island, it raised around £18,000, and I was able to show the public that I was fully fit. My omission from the Test side caused a furore throughout the Caribbean. Politicians made speeches about it, and sixty-four sportsmen petitioned the Trinidadian Prime Minister, Dr Eric Williams, to have the matter brought up at the Heads of Government Conference in Guyana.

Dr Williams, whom I had met on previous occasions, deplored the way the Board handled the matter in a speech at the Naparima Bowl.

> If I could speak for my colleagues on this issue, if it was a political matter, we would never have thought of proceeding without asking the views of the persons concerned. I happen to be one of those people, thousands of them in the West Indies and outside the West Indies, who believe that Mr Sobers is one of the authentic folk-heroes produced by the West Indian people.
>
> I would like to utter my regret as head of Government in Trinidad and Tobago that if there had been some difficulty the impression should have been left behind that Mr Sobers should have been dealt with just as if it was in typical West Indian fashion we were discarding at the wayside an old car that had been smashed up in a road accident. . . . I regret it. If I had been involved in any way, it would have been handled differently.

Ian Chappell, the Australian captain, commented to the press: 'If we win this series against a West Indies team which does not include Garry Sobers it will be a hollow victory.'

I was mad at the time, but there is no bitterness now. I am not a man to live with animosity. Handled differently, there would have been no problem. Bernard Julien from Trinidad was brought in for the Barbados Test, but the day before the match was struck on the arm and broke a bone. Another Barbadian, Keith Boyce, took over. Julien was one of several West Indian players with ability and potential who never fully fulfilled them. Lawrence Rowe and Alvin Kallicharran were two others.

Kallicharran played 66 Tests in all and averaged 44, and though I did not play a lot with him he always struck me as being a little too arrogant. He tried to copy Rohan Kanhai in his ways. They spent much time together. I would try to talk to him, but he would take more notice of Rohan.

The Chappell brothers and Doug Walters dominated a strong Australian batting side on that tour. Greg was to finish with a better record than his brother in Tests, but I always felt Ian was more the man for a crisis. Greg made a pile of runs, yet never convinced me he relished playing the fast bowlers. Doug Walters was an outstanding hard-wicket player. He liked the ball coming on to the bat. In England, where the pitches were slower, he usually failed.

The Australians had a sound pair of openers in Keith Stackpole and Ian Redpath. Stackpole was a brilliant hooker. Redpath was steadier, straighter. I was not the only West Indian player to be in the middle of a selection controversy for that series. The Trinidadian batsman Charlie Davis, so successful the two previous years, was omitted for the first three Tests, which upset the Trinidadians, and when the Board declined to pay for Clive Lloyd to come home from Australia where he was playing club cricket the Guyanese Prime Minister paid for Lloyd to come home himself.

Clive played the final three Tests, scored 178 in Guyana much to the delight of Forbes Burnham, and finished top of the West Indian batting averages. The series was a miserable one for the West Indies. There had been too much discord, too many unnecessary rows.

After the West Indies versus Australia series, the West Indies were scheduled to play three Tests in England in 1973, and I was asked if I would be available. I realised that I would not be able to play

English county cricket much longer because of its increasing demands and replied that I felt I owed something to Nottinghamshire, who had not seen as much of me as they were entitled to after signing me for a big fee in 1968. My first duty, I said, was to Nottinghamshire but I would be available for the Test matches only. Mr Marley said the Board would accept that.

After my début for Nottinghamshire in 1968, when I helped them advance to fourth in the championship table from fifteenth the previous season, I missed half the 1969 season because of a West Indies tour, half the 1970 season through the Rest of the World series and most of the 1972 season because of my knee injury.

Early in the 1973 tour by Rohan Kanhai's side, the manager, Esmond Kentish, the former Jamaican fast bowler, rang me and said: 'Garry, what's the position? Do you want to play?' That rattled me slightly. 'What kind of question is that?' I said. 'I already told the selectors I am available for the Tests. I will play, but don't ask me if I wanted to play. If I fail, they will say: "But he wanted to play." It's a question of whether the Board want me to play. If picked, I will play and promise that I will give one hundred per cent as I have always done.'

No one asked me to see a doctor or justify my fitness. My form with Nottinghamshire barely justified a Test call-up. There was pressure on me. People would be looking closer to see just how fit I was after the dispute in March and April.

I felt in good shape when I turned up for the First Test at the Oval. I made 10 and 51, and the West Indies won by 158 runs, chiefly owing to the splendid pace bowling of Keith Boyce whose 11 for 147 was more wickets in a Test than any West Indian had previously recorded.

I have written about the Birmingham Test, a thoroughly disagreeable affair, and also the victory by an innings and 226 runs at Lord's when I scored an unbeaten, interrupted 150 not out in my final Test appearance at cricket's most famous ground.

Less than six months later the two teams were back in action in the Caribbean with the Kent skipper Mike Denness leading England in place of Illingworth. It was to be my last Test series. At thirty-seven I no longer needed any glory. I had had enough of that. Nor did I need the hassle from being in the public eye all the time. Before I resigned as captain, I led the West Indies in 39 consecutive Tests and must have been interviewed by hundreds of newspaper, television and radio men.

I loved playing cricket and the social life attached to it, but being exposed to so much press attention was one side of it I did not enjoy. Too many of my words were distorted by journalists with their views interspersed with mine and provocative headlines put on the stories. I was in more trouble from what was written about me than from anything else in my career. It was the same anywhere I went in the world.

Not all the journalists were like that. I had great respect for the late Ray Robinson in Australia. He would always tell you what he was going to write and seek your reaction before it went into print. Some of the others would take a chance and hope I didn't mind. I wasn't a regular reader of newspapers. When a provocative article appeared, it was always shown to me by someone else. Another reporter I admired was the late Ron Roberts in England. Ron used to take touring sides abroad and, like Ray Robinson, knew the game intimately and loved it.

I recognise that the press performs a much needed public-relations function for cricket, but I wish some if its members would be more responsible in their writings. They were too quick to write players down and say they were finished without understanding why they had failed in a particular match or series. There was too little sympathy shown, too little understanding.

The West Indies were the better side in the series against Denness's side, yet were held to a 1–1 draw. The player who did most to achieve that surprising result was Tony Greig, who established himself as a world-class all-rounder with 430 runs, average 47, and 24 wickets at 22 apiece. In his medium-fast style, Greig was an underrated bowler.

No bowler takes 141 Test wickets without having some ability. Greig was an experimenter. He was always willing to try something different to take a wicket, even if it was a bad ball. This led to some of our batsmen taking him too lightly, particularly in the final match at Port of Spain which England won to level the series with Greig taking 13 wickets for 156 runs. The West Indies needed 226 to win, and it should have been well within our capabilities.

Players were saying: 'He can't bowl. I'll show him.' And they went out and threw the bat and got out to him. I kept telling them to calm down, but no one would listen. In that match Greig was bowling in his slower style. The press said he was bowling off-breaks, but he wasn't. He was bowling off-cutters, and with his height they had to be watched carefully. Five batsmen passed 20, yet no one reached 50. That was our problem: no one played an innings.

Greig had me caught for 0 in the first innings, and I was determined not to end my Test career with a first ever 'pair'. I came in planning to act as the anchor man. Deryck Murray helped me take the score to 135–6 when Derek Underwood bowled me a rare full toss. Derek didn't like bowling against left-handers, like most bowlers, and he bowled an occasional loose ball against me. Instead of playing it naturally, I was a little too careful, trying to find the gap, and missed. Bowled by a full toss for 20 in my last Test innings!

Greig was also a brilliant, intimidating fielder, and his enthusiasm sometimes led him into trouble. The much publicised incident in the First Test in Port of Spain, when he ran out Kallicharran off the last ball of the day, caused the authorities to meet and reverse the umpires' decision because of the fear of more rioting.

Kalli had rescued the innings and was 142 not out. Julien played the last ball of the day safely down to Greig at silly point, Alan Knott pulled out the stumps at that end and Kallicharran started to walk towards the dressing-room. Umpire Douglas Sang Hue, however, had not called 'Over', so technically Greig was within his rights to throw down the wicket Kallicharran's end. When Greig appealed, the umpire had no alternative but to give Kalli out.

The crowd were puzzled at first, then angry when they realised that Kalli was out. Both managers met afterwards with Board officials, and three hours later emerged to read a statement which said: 'Whilst appreciating that this is not strictly within the laws of cricket, the England manager and captain have, in the interests of cricket as a whole and the future of this tour in particular, requested that the appeal be withdrawn.' The umpires agreed, and a potentially explosive situation was averted.

I had a drink in the dressing-room with Greig that evening. He was worried that the crowd might set upon him when he left, so I said I would return to his hotel with him. There were few people outside when we came out, and he was not molested. I told him he had no reason to be apologetic. 'Kalli is a young, inexperienced player. It was his fault for leaving his ground before the umpire called "Over".'

The other player who saved England on that tour was Dennis Amiss, the Warwickshire opening batsman who scored 663 runs, average 82. Dennis made six centuries on the tour, three in the Tests, including an innings of 262 not out.

He was a much more adventurous player than his partner Geoff Boycott. While Geoff accumulated runs, not taking the slightest chance, Dennis played his shots, particularly in front of the wicket on the off side. He was also strong through mid-wicket. West Indian spectators liked him. He was their type of player. Julien and Boyce were our quickest bowlers at the time, and on flat pitches he found little difficulty batting for long periods.

In Australia less than a year later, he discovered Lillee and Jeff Thomson were much harder to handle. He fractured a thumb in the First Test, and his confidence was so affected that he had recorded a 'pair' by the end of a disappointing series. His experiences in Australia persuaded him to open up his stance against the quicker bowlers, and he managed to overcome his problems. He should have gone on and scored many more runs for England, but I think going to join Kerry Packer's World Series Cricket ruined his career at international level.

One of England's successful batsmen on the 1973–4 tour of the West Indies was Keith Fletcher of Essex. Keith looked a world-beater, a batsman with a full range of shots. But he never really became a Test regular. Nor did John Jameson, who also went on that tour. John was in the Colin Milburn mould, a very aggressive opening batsman who loved hitting sixes. I don't think the English selectors like aggressive opening batsmen!

That series saw the début of one of the greatest bowlers ever developed in the West Indies: Andy Roberts, the first Antiguan to be selected. As he became older, so he became craftier. He was always fast, frighteningly fast on quick pitches.

Years of experience in England with Hampshire taught him to cut his pace down and vary his bowling. Some people say fast bowlers burn themselves out playing seven days a week in England. Andy showed that an intelligent bowler can profit from the time in England and make himself a better bowler. He learned to move the ball and bowl different types of bouncer. He rarely strayed from a good line, and no batsman could relax against him.

When that series ended, I returned to Nottinghamshire for my final season and announced it would be my last. The press wrote that I was retiring from first-class cricket! I never said anything about retiring from first-class cricket! I still planned to play for Barbados. First, I thought I would take some time out and have a rest and play some golf. Maybe in two years I could make a comeback. That did not happen.

I had resigned as captain of Nottinghamshire, and the club appointed Jack Bond, the former Lancashire skipper, now an umpire. I would have liked to have done more for the county in my last season but, although I came top of the batting averages (1110 runs, average 48), I only took 29 wickets. The highlight was a century in eighty-three minutes against Derby at Ilkeston, the fastest of the season. It won me the Lawrence Trophy as well as the National Sporting Club's prize.

The following season I played for Littleborough in the Central Lancashire League, becoming one of two professionals who passed 1000 runs and took 68 wickets. The other was Australia's Trevor Chappell.

While at Littleborough I was asked by the West Indies Board if I was available for the first Prudential World Cup, the final of which was taking place at Lord's. I would have loved to play. It would have been a fitting climax to my career. But I told Clyde Walcott I had pulled a muscle and, though it might have healed in the intervening two weeks, I did not believe it was worth taking the risk.

Countries had to declare their fourteen players in advance, and if someone dropped out there was no provision to call up a replacement. Clyde accepted my decision, and Rohan Kanhai was asked to play instead. At thirty-eight, I think I could have played more cricket. But the travelling and the hassle had taken their toll. It was time to go. Golf, with its different, more private pressures, had taken over. I would not like to think I left cricket in any bitterness. I enjoyed my twenty years at the top. It was a great life.

After a spell working for CARICOM, the federation of Caribbean nations, I am now employed by the Barbados Tourist Board. My boss is the Minister of Tourism and Sport, Wesley Winfield Hall. We still talk cricket and we would both love to be still playing.

Neither of my sons, Matthew aged sixteen, and Daniel who is thirteen, is keen on cricket. That does not worry me. They have to make their own careers without me pushing them. They are living with me now in Barbados, and my wife Pru has our daughter, Genevieve, age nine, in Melbourne. It is no secret that Pru and I are separated. That is a sad part of my life, that my marriage eventually failed, but it lasted sixteen years and not many people said it would last!

I met Pru when she was working as a public relations girl with the Australian Canned Fruit Industry. She came to Trent Bridge to ask me to tape a message to promote Australian fruit. Naturally I accepted. Pretty blondes don't come up to you and ask you to send messages to Australia every day. That night she accepted my invitation to have a drink, and the relationship started from that day. We were married in England in September 1969.

When World Series Cricket started in Australia we moved house from Nottingham to Melbourne, and I was there seven years working in various coaching and promotional capacities. I liked Australia and its people. They are very genuine people. But it was always my intention to return to Barbados some day.

Pru wanted to stay in Melbourne, her home town. She probably tired of my travelling and gambling. By this time she was writing and promoting a book of her own and was having a successful career and did not want to live in Barbados. We agreed to go our own ways. These things happen in life. Matthew and Daniel are at good schools where the discipline is sound, and I have no fears about their education.

Around the end of 1974 I had a message from someone at the British High Commission in Barbados saying the High Commissioner wanted to see me. He said I had been recommended for a knighthood and wanted to know whether I was willing to accept. Two other cricketers from the West Indies have been knighted by Her Majesty the Queen: Sir Learie, later Lord, Constantine and Sir Frank Worrell.

I was tremendously flattered. It was an honour for me, for Barbados and for West Indies cricket, and it meant that I was being recognised as a good ambassador of my sport around the world. I promised to think the matter over and next day telephoned the High Commissioner to say I would be delighted to accept. I was told to keep the news quiet, but soon everyone in Barbados seemed to know.

The Prime Minister, Errol Barrow, provided a party for me and during the evening announced that I was to become Sir Garfield Sobers. Two friends from the world of show business, Tom Jones and Engelbert Humperdinck, were present. I knew Engelbert from the days I used to visit the Cromford Club, a club frequented by sportsmen in Manchester. Engelbert used to sing there, and he was known as Gerry Dorsey then.

I believe it was the former British Prime Minister, Harold Wilson, who recommended me for the knighthood. He was keen on cricket through his friendship with Fred Trueman, and I had met him on a number of occasions and got on well with him.

The official ceremony took place in February 1975 at the Garrison in Barbados when the Queen came to the island to open the National Insurance Building. There were around 10,000 people there, and it was a day I will never forget. As the Queen placed the sword on each shoulder, Matthew, aged four, said: 'What's the lady doing putting that stick on Daddy's shoulder?'

I was happy for my mother and family, those 'father figures' of my youth and all those who had supported me and helped me on the way to the top. I knew they were all sharing this very special moment with me.

I joined Sir Learie, Sir Frank and one Australian, Sir Donald Bradman, and four Englishmen, Sir Pelham Warner, Sir Jack Hobbs, Sir Len Hutton and Sir George Allen, as the eight cricketers to be knighted for their services to cricket. It was a proud moment. It happened about a mile from where I was born. Who would have thought that a poor boy from a wooden house in Walcott Avenue would end up like this?

Appendix | Test Career Statistics

(Courtesy of *Wisden Cricketers' Almanack*)

Batting for West Indies

Season	Against	Tests	Inns	Not Outs	Runs	Highest Inns	100s	50s	Average	Catches
1933–4	England	1	2	0	40	26	0	0	40.00	0
1955	Australia	4	8	2	231	64	0	1	38.50	1
1956	New Zealand	4	5	0	81	27	0	0	16.20	5
1957	England	5	10	0	320	66	0	2	32.00	1
1957–8	Pakistan	5	8	2	824	365*	3	3	137.33	2
1958–9	India	5	8	2	557	198	3	0	92.83	5
1958–9	Pakistan	3	5	0	160	72	0	1	32.00	2
1959–60	England	5	8	1	709	226	3	1	101.28	7
1960–1	Australia	5	10	0	430	168	2	1	43.00	12
1962	India	5	7	1	424	153	2	1	70.66	11
1963	England	5	8	0	322	102	1	2	40.25	8
1965	Australia	5	10	1	352	69	0	2	39.11	8
1966	England	5	8	1	722	174	3	2	103.14	10
1966–7	India	3	5	2	342	95	0	5	114.00	7
1967–8	England	5	9	3	545	152	2	2	90.83	4
1968–9	Australia	5	10	0	497	113	2	2	49.70	6
1968–9	New Zealand	3	5	0	70	39	0	0	14.00	5
1969	England	3	6	1	150	50*	0	1	30.00	2
1971	India	5	10	2	597	178*	3	0	74.62	4
1971–2	New Zealand	5	8	1	253	142	1	0	36.14	2
1973	England	3	5	1	306	150*	1	2	76.50	7
1974	England	4	5	0	100	57	0	1	20.00	1
Totals		93	160	21	8032	365*	26	30	57.78	110

Mode of Dismissal: Bowled 34, caught 79, lbw 16, stumped 1, run out 9. Total 139.

* Indicates not out.

Bowling for West Indies

Season	Against	Matches	Balls	Maidens	Runs	Wickets	5 wkts in Innings	Average
1953–4	England	1	179	9	81	4	0	20.25
1955	Australia	4	563	36	213	6	0	35.50
1956	New Zealand	4	281	26	49	2	0	24.50
1957	England	5	804	24	355	5	0	71.00
1957–8	Pakistan	5	1029	53	377	4	0	94.25
1958–9	India	5	715	33	292	10	0	29.20
1958–9	Pakistan	3	396	36	77	0	0	–
1959–60	England	5	684	14	355	9	0	39.44
1960–1	Australia	5	1528	27	588	15	1	39.20
1962	India	5	1341	61	473	23	1	20.56
1963	England	5	1386	50	571	20	1	28.55
1965	Australia	5	1155	53	490	12	0	40.83
1966	England	5	1618	78	545	20	1	27.25
1966–7	India	3	931	51	350	14	0	25.00
1967–8	England	5	1397	72	508	13	0	39.07
1968–9	Australia	5	1649	37	733	18	1	40.72
1968–9	New Zealand	3	840	23	301	7	0	43.00
1969	England	3	870	47	318	11	1	28.90
1971	India	5	1314	71	401	12	0	33.41
1971–2	New Zealand	5	1086	56	332	10	0	33.20
1973	England	3	493	24	169	6	0	28.16
1974	England	4	1340	92	421	14	0	30.07
	Totals	93	21599	973	7999	235	6	34.03

How wickets were taken: bowled 54; caught 137; lbw 38; stumped 6; total 235.

Batting for West Indies

	Tests	Inns	Not Outs	Runs	Highest Inns	100s	50s	Average	Catches
v. England	36	61	8	3214	174	10	13	60.64	40
v. Australia	19	38	3	1510	168	4	6	43.14	27
v. New Zealand	12	18	1	404	142	1	0	23.76	12
v. India	18	30	7	1920	198	8	7	83.47	27
v. Pakistan	8	13	2	984	365*	3	4	89.45	4
Totals	93	160	21	8032	365*	26	30	57.78	110

* Indicates not out

Bowling for West Indies

	Tests	Balls	Maidens	Runs	Wickets	5 wkts in Inns	Average
England	36	8771	410	3323	102	3	32.57
Australia	19	4895	153	2024	51	2	39.68
New Zealand	12	2207	105	682	19	0	35.89
India	18	4301	216	1516	59	1	25.69
Pakistan	8	1425	89	454	4	0	113.50
Totals	93	21599	973	7999	235	6	34.03

Batting for West Indies

	Tests	Inns	Not Outs	Runs	Highest Inns	100s	50s	Average	Catches
in West Indies	44	75	14	4075	365*	14	12	66.80	40
in Australia	10	20	0	927	168	4	3	46.35	18
in England	21	37	3	1820	174	5	9	53.52	28
in India	8	13	4	899	198	3	5	99.88	12
in New Zealand	7	10	0	151	39	0	0	15.10	10
in Pakistan	3	5	0	160	72	0	1	32.00	2
Totals	93	160	21	8032	365*	26	30	57.78	110

Bowling for West Indies

	Tests	Balls	Maidens	Runs	Wickets	5 wkts in Inns	Average
West Indies	44	10088	517	3651	107	1	34.12
Australia	10	3177	64	1321	33	2	40.03
England	21	5171	223	1958	62	3	31.58
India	8	1646	84	642	24	0	26.75
New Zealand	7	1121	49	350	9	0	38.88
Pakistan	3	396	36	77	0	0	–
Totals	93	21599	973	7999	235	6	34.03

Batting on West Indian Grounds

Ground	Tests	Inns	Not Outs	Runs	Highest Inns	100s	50s	Average	Catches
Bridgetown	9	14	2	914	226	3	3	76.16	9
Georgetown	7	12	3	853	145	5	1	94.77	5
Kingston	11	18	5	1354	365*	5	4	104.15	8
Port of Spain	17	31	4	954	132	1	4	35.33	18
Totals	44	75	14	4075	365*	14	12	66.80	40

Batting on Australian Grounds

Ground	Tests	Inns	Not Outs	Runs	Highest Inns	100s	50s	Average	Catches
Adelaide	2	4	0	183	110	1	1	45.75	4
Brisbane	2	4	0	184	132	1	0	46.00	4
Melbourne	3	6	0	180	67	0	2	30.00	6
Sydney	3	6	0	380	168	2	0	63.33	4
Totals	10	20	0	927	168	4	3	46.35	18

Batting on English Grounds

Ground	Tests	Inns	Not Outs	Runs	Highest Inns	100s	50s	Average	Catches
Edgbaston	3	6	0	190	74	0	2	31.66	2
Headingley	4	7	0	374	174	2	1	53.42	2
Lord's	5	9	3	571	163*	2	2	95.16	8
Old Trafford	3	4	0	283	161	1	1	70.75	8
The Oval	4	7	0	249	81	0	2	35.57	3
Trent Bridge	2	4	0	153	94	0	1	38.25	5
Totals	21	37	3	1820	174	5	9	53.52	28

Batting on Indian Grounds

Ground	Tests	Inns	Not Outs	Runs	Highest Inns	100s	50s	Average	Catches
Bombay	2	4	2	270	142*	1	2	135.00	5
Calcutta	2	2	1	176	106*	1	1	176.00	2
Kanpur	1	2	0	202	198	1	0	101.00	0
Madras	2	4	1	207	95	0	2	69.00	5
New Delhi	1	1	0	44	44	0	0	44.00	0
Totals	8	13	4	899	198	3	5	99.88	12

Batting on New Zealand Grounds

Ground	Tests	Inns	Not Outs	Runs	Highest Inns	100s	50s	Average	Catches
Auckland	2	4	0	13	11	0	0	3.25	3
Christchurch	2	2	0	25	25	0	0	12.50	2
Dunedin	1	1	0	27	27	0	0	27.00	2
Wellington	2	3	0	86	39	0	0	28.66	3
Totals	7	10	0	151	39	0	0	15.10	10

Batting on Pakistan Grounds

Ground	Tests	Inns	Not Outs	Runs	Highest Inns	100s	50s	Average	Catches
Dacca	1	2	0	74	45	0	0	37.00	0
Karachi	1	2	0	14	14	0	0	7.00	0
Lahore	1	1	0	72	72	0	1	72.00	2
Totals	3	5	0	160	72	0	1	32.00	2

Bowling on West Indian Grounds

Ground	Tests	Balls	Maidens	Runs	Wickets	5 wkts in Inns	Average
Bridgetown	9	2159	125	761	19	0	40.05
Georgetown	7	1680	94	577	20	0	28.85
Kingston	11	2390	116	879	27	1	32.55
Port of Spain	17	3859	182	1434	41	0	34.97
Totals	44	10088	517	3651	107	1	34.12

Bowling on Australian Grounds

Ground	Tests	Balls	Maidens	Runs	Wickets	5 wkts in Inns	Average
Adelaide	2	904	19	364	7	0	52.00
Brisbane	2	702	17	248	9	1	27.55
Melbourne	3	859	14	337	10	1	33.70
Sydney	3	712	14	372	7	0	53.14
Totals	10	3177	64	1321	33	2	40.03

Bowling on English Grounds

Ground	Tests	Balls	Maidens	Runs	Wickets	5 wkts in Inns	Average
Edgbaston	3	750	25	300	10	1	30.00
Headingley	4	1024	42	374	19	2	19.68
Lord's	5	858	42	340	7	0	48.57
Old Trafford	3	822	35	338	8	0	42.25
The Oval	4	1111	55	385	12	0	32.08
Trent Bridge	2	606	24	221	6	0	36.83
Totals	21	5171	223	1958	62	3	31.58

Bowling on Indian Grounds

Ground	Tests	Balls	Maidens	Runs	Wickets	5 wkts in Inns	Average
Bombay	2	348	15	152	5	0	30.40
Calcutta	2	341	18	141	9	0	15.66
Kanpur	1	270	14	91	2	0	45.50
Madras	2	543	34	192	8	0	24.00
New Delhi	1	144	3	66	0	0	–
Totals	8	1646	84	642	24	0	26.75

Bowling on New Zealand Grounds

Ground	Tests	Balls	Maidens	Runs	Wickets	5 wkts in Inns	Average
Auckland	2	512	15	201	3	0	67.00
Christchurch	2	312	11	91	3	0	30.33
Dunedin	1	24	4	0	0	0	–
Wellington	2	273	19	58	3	0	19.33
Totals	7	1121	49	350	9	0	38.88

Bowling on Pakistan Grounds

Ground	Tests	Balls	Maidens	Runs	Wickets	5 wkts in Inns	Average
Dacca	1	66	6	11	0	0	–
Karachi	1	294	29	57	0	0	–
Lahore	1	36	1	9	0	0	–
Totals	3	396	36	77	0	0	–

Centuries (26)

v. Australia (4)
132 at Brisbane, 1960–1
168 at Sydney, 1960–1
110 at Adelaide, 1968–9
113 at Sydney, 1968–9

v. England (10)
226 at Bridgetown, 1959–60
147 at Kingston, 1959–60
145 at Georgetown, 1959–60
102 at Headingley, 1963
161 at Old Trafford, 1966
163* at Lord's, 1966
174 at Headingley, 1966
113* at Kingston, 1967–8
152 at Georgetown, 1967–8
150* at Lord's 1973

v. India (8)
142* at Bombay, 1958–9
198 at Kanpur, 1958–9
106* at Calcutta, 1958–9
153 at Kingston, 1962
104 at Kingston, 1962
108* at Georgetown, 1971
178* at Bridgetown, 1971
132 at Port of Spain, 1971

v. New Zealand (1)
142 at Bridgetown, 1971–2

v. Pakistan (3)
365* at Kingston, 1957–8
125 at Georgetown, 1957–8
(1st Innings)
109* at Georgetown, 1957–8
(2nd Innings)

Indicates not out

Wicket Partnerships in Which G. S. Sobers Has Shared

179 for 4th wicket with C. L. Walcott v. Australia at Kingston, 1955
100 for 5th wicket with E. D. Weekes v. England at Lord's, 1957
446 for 2nd wicket with C. C. Hunte v. Pakistan at Kingston, 1957–8
269 for 2nd wicket with C. L. Walcott v. Pakistan at Georgetown, 1957–8
188* for 4th wicket with C. L. Walcott v. Pakistan at Kingston, 1957–8
135 for 2nd wicket with C. C. Hunte v. Pakistan at Georgetown, 1957–8
101 for 5th wicket with O. G. Smith v. Pakistan at Port of Spain, 1957–8
119 for 4th wicket with O. G. Smith v. India at Bombay, 1958–9
134* for 5th wicket with B. F. Butcher v. India at Bombay, 1958–9
114 for 5th wicket with B. F. Butcher v. India at Kanpur, 1958–9
163 for 6th wicket with J. Solomon v. India at Kanpur, 1958–9
160* for 6th wicket with J. Solomon v. India at Calcutta, 1958–9

162 for 3rd wicket with R. B. Kanhai v. Pakistan at Lahore, 1958–9

399 for 4th wicket with F. M. Worrell v. England at Bridgetown, 1959–60

115 for 3rd wicket with R. B. Kanhai v. England at Georgetown, 1959–60

121 for 5th wicket with F. M. Worrell v. England at Georgetown, 1959–60

133 for 3rd wicket with E. McMorris v. England at Kingston, 1959–60
(McMorris retired hurt and the stand continued with S. M. Nurse for 110 more runs)

174 for 4th wicket with F. M. Worrell v. Australia at Brisbane, 1960–1

128 for 5th wicket with S. M. Nurse v. Australia at Sydney, 1960–1

110 for 6th wicket with F. M. Worrell v. India at Kingston, 1962

127 for 7th wicket with I. Mendonca v. India at Kingston, 1962

120 for 4th wicket with C. C. Hunte v. England at Old Trafford, 1963

143 for 4th wicket with R. B. Kanhai v. England at Headingley, 1963

160 for 4th wicket with B. F. Butcher v. Australia at Port of Spain, 1965

127 for 6th wicket with D. A. J. Holford v. England at Old Trafford, 1966

274* for 6th wicket with D. A. J. Holford v. England at Lord's, 1966

173 for 5th wicket with B. F. Butcher v. England at Trent Bridge, 1966

265 for 5th wicket with S. M. Nurse v. England at Headingley, 1966

122 for 5th wicket with R. B. Kanhai v. England at The Oval, 1966

102* for 5th wicket with C. H. Lloyd v. India at Bombay, 1966–7

110 for 6th wicket with D. A. J. Holford v. England at Kingston, 1967–8

63* for 9th wicket with W. W. Hall v. England at Port of Spain, 1967–8

250 for 4th wicket with R. B. Kanhai v. England at Georgetown, 1967–8

134 for 5th wicket with S. M. Nurse v. Australia at Melbourne, 1968–9

118 for 6th wicket with S. M. Nurse v. Australia at Sydney, 1968–9

173 for 4th wicket with R. B. Kanhai v. India at Kingston, 1971

170* for 4th wicket with C. A. Davis v. India at Georgetown, 1971

167 for 4th wicket with C. A. Davis v. India at Bridgetown, 1971

107* for 6th wicket with J. N. Shepherd v. India at Bridgetown, 1971

177 for 5th wicket with C. A. Davis v. India at Port of Spain, 1971

254   for 6th wicket with C. A. Davis v. New Zealand at Bridgetown, 1971–2
155* for 7th wicket with B. D. Julien v. England at Lord's, 1973 (Sobers retired and the stand continued with K. D. Boyce for 76 more runs)
112   for 6th wicket with B. D. Julien v. England at Kingston, 1974

* *stand unfinished*

Best Bowling

5 for 120 runs v. Australia at Melbourne, 1960–1
5 for 63 runs v. India at Kingston, 1962
5 for 60 runs v. England at Edgbaston, 1963
5 for 41 runs v. England at Headingley, 1966
6 for 73 runs v. Australia at Brisbane, 1968–9
5 for 42 runs v. England at Headingley, 1969

For the Rest of the World v. England, 1970

Batting

Matches	Inns	Not Outs	Runs	Highest Inns	100s	50s	Average	Catches
5	9	1	588	183	2	3	73.50	7

Bowling

Matches	Balls	Maidens	Runs	Wickets	5 wkts in Innings	Average
5	1636	106	452	21	1	21.52

Centuries (2)

183 at Lord's

114 at Headingley

Best Partnerships

198 for 7th wicket with Intikhab Alam at Lord's

155 for 5th wicket with C. H. Lloyd at Edgbaston

165 for 5th wicket with R. G. Pollock at The Oval

Best Bowling

6 for 21 runs at Lord's

Sobers's Full Record in Test Cricket

Batting

Matches	Inns	Not Outs	Runs	Highest Inns	100s	50s	Average	Catches
98	169	22	8620	365*	28	33	58.63	117

Bowling

Matches	Balls	Maidens	Runs	Wickets	5 wkts in Innings	Average
98	23235	1079	8451	256	7	33.01

Index

Picture Acknowledgements

Section 1 Page 2 above, Author's Collection. Page 2 below, 3, 6, 8, Tony Cozier. Page 1, 7, Patrick Eagar. Page 4, Keystone Collection. Page 5, Sport and General Press Agency.

Section 2 Page 15 above left, *The Age*, Melbourne. Page 13 above left, 15 above right, Willie Alleyne. Page 15 below, 16 below, Author's Collection. Page 11 above right, 14 below, Tony Cozier. Page 16 above right, Daily Mirror/Syndication International/photo Dennis Hussey. Page 9, 10 below, 12 above, Patrick Eagar. Page 12 below, Vernon Fung. Page 14 above, Glamour Photo Service/photo D. Bushell. Page 10 above, 11 above left and below, 12 centre, 13 below, 16 above left, Sport and General Press Agency. Page 13 above right, Sydney Morning Herald.

The publishers have endeavoured to acknowledge all known persons holding copyright or reproduction rights for the illustrations in this book.

Frances Edmonds
Cricket XXXX Cricket £2.99

By the bestselling author of *Another Bloody Tour*

After three months Down Under, Frances Edmonds had done a lot more than watch England retain the Ashes and avoid the rigours of the British winter.

Since cricket bores her immeasurably, Frances had time to take in The Melbourne Cup ('Ascot, the Derby and Henley rolled into one'), and the America's Cup – where she met Harold Cudmore and the crew of the *White Crusader*.

She also had a job – hosting Channel 10 TV's morning programme – that is until her outrageous sense of humour got her the sack and left the Channel's telephone exchange on meltdown.

Frances, however, loves Australia, and Australia, by all accounts, loves Frances. She was the first woman to address two Lord's Taverners' luncheons, and she was invited to Canberra to speak to the National Press Club on Australia Day.

Cricket XXXX Cricket is a wickedly irreverent book, and one of the great victories of the Australian Tour.

'Shocking, witty and perceptive . . . appealing to cricket haters and devotees alike' THE SUNDAY EXPRESS

'The book is packed with irresistible stories and very funny anecdotes; the saga of the obscene gingernut limerick . . . and the tale of the Gucci-clad kangaroo are "beauts".' PUBLISHING NEWS

Dick Francis
The Sport of Queens £3.50

The autobiography of the champion steeplechase jockey who became an internationally acclaimed thriller writer

'I learned to ride when I was five, on a donkey . . .'

So begins Dick Francis's enthralling autobiography. His elder brother had bet him sixpence that he could not jump a fence on the stubborn animal. After several tries, Francis managed to steer the creature over. 'In my heart, from that moment, I became a professional horseman'.

Dick Francis, known around the world as the creator of a whole string of bestselling thrillers, has always set them against the background he knows so intimately – the colourful and endlessly fascinating world of the turf. *The Sport of Queens* traces the Francis story from the early days of showjumping, through his war service in the Royal Air Force and his meteoric career as one of Britain's leading National Hunt jockeys and champion steeplechasers – and jockey to the Queen Mother – to the transition from riding to writing winners. It is a lively and thoroughly entertaining story, written with verve, humour and unassumed modesty.

'Francis has plenty to tell – and he tells it very well'
HORSE AND HOUND

'Sheer enchantment' SPORTING CHRONICLE

All Dick Francis's thrillers are available in Pan.